Celebration
Circles

Celebration Circles

A Guide for
Celebrating
&
Honoring
People & Events
in our Lives

Nancy McCreight and Sherry Winter

Published by Celebration Circles
P.O. Box 283
Princeton, MN 55371

Contents

What Drew Us To Circle

Nancy:

Think about times in your life when you were with others and you felt listened to, your voice was acknowledged and differences were honored. I feel fortunate when I experience this type of gathering with friends or family sharing stories or working with others on a collaborative project.

In 1997 I was drawn to be part of a community-based restorative justice program where I met my co-author, Sherry. We were introduced to peacemaking circles used in the Yukon, Canada to help communities restore the harm caused by crime. I am grateful to those who brought circle to our community: Harold Gatensby, Mark Wedge, Kay Pranis and Barry Stuart.

While restorative justice was the focus, I soon realized my experience in these circles was much more. In the circle, respect and listening for understanding were paramount. It felt very different from most other groups. The experience and skills of each person, regardless of her/his title, were acknowledged and considered.

Many of us drawn to the project to help strengthen our community found we were personally changed by the experience. We wanted the essence of the circle, respectfully sharing stories and learning from each other, to continue. Together we have planned many circles and I am always amazed and inspired by each circle, whether it be a birthday celebration, a house warming, or a celebration of nature.

This book was born from these experiences that have so enriched my life. It is about the wonder and joy of celebrating and honoring each other. The circle process is truly a gift to share with others as it was shared with me.

Sherry:

Participating in the circle process became a catalyst for change in my life. As owner and operator of fast food establishments for twenty-seven years, life had been about how much work I could extract from others and myself. What I was missing was the ability to slow down, truly listen to myself and embrace the presence of others. Circles became a place where I found my voice, a place where my spirit could come home to.

My first circle experience was a four day training with Mark Wedge and Harold Gatensby from the Yukon for implementing Peacemaking Circles in our community. We learned that circles are a way of gathering where each participant has an equal voice, is respected and truly heard. We were to trust our instincts, respect each other's values and share leadership. This was an appealing concept! People actually took turns to speak and everyone else listened. I had never experienced this in a group before. I was hooked.

That weekend was the beginning of my search to experience the circle way of communicating and connecting with others. Training with Christina Baldwin and Ann Linnea of PeerSpirit and the staff at The Ojai Foundation gave me insight as to how this process could be applied in many different settings and with participants from any age or stage of life.

The journey since my introduction to circle has been one of personal growth and joy. It has led to hosting circles that celebrate and honor our place in the universe. The simple act of preparing space for a circle gathering is transformational for me. I instantly sense the beauty of sharing stories and honoring each other's journeys and the connectedness we will create together.

Book Overview

Our book will help you plan a circle for any occasion. Is there a special person or a group you would like to honor? Is there a time of year or holiday you want to celebrate in a different way? Maybe there is a rite of passage you, or someone you know, is going through that would be enriched by a gathering that includes some ceremony and sharing of stories. Or perhaps just taking time to appreciate nature or express gratitude for what life has brought is a reason to create a circle gathering.

In *Celebration Circles*, we describe in detail how to plan and hold a circle. We begin with "The Power of Circle" which reveals why circle gatherings create a powerful and respectful space for sharing our stories and honoring what holds meaning in our lives. In "Circle Stories," you hear the voices of people who have been in circle as they reflect on their experiences. These stories give you ideas for the many ways circles can be used. Following the circle stories are simple guidelines for "Planning a Circle" and "Holding a Circle."

In the next section of our book, "Circle Themes," we developed 48 different circles that range from traditional celebrations, such as birthdays and anniversaries, to honoring a milestone in life and celebrating the solstices. The 48 circles are grouped under six different themes: Connections, Beginnings, Discovery, Transitions, The Journey, and The World Around Us. At the beginning of each theme, we include a circle story that ties in with the group of circles we developed for that theme.

"Circles in Other Settings" follows and shows how circle can be used in schools and the workplace and includes sample circles for those settings. In the "Appendix," we include ideas for activities, sample invitations, and additional comments about planning and hosting a circle. The last section of our book, "Circle Resources" suggests other books that help in planning a circle and provides resources to learn more about the many ways circle has and can be used.

Join us as we share our experiences of circle and explore ways it can be used to celebrate and honor our lives and stories. We invite you to draw on your life experiences to create meaningful gatherings that embrace and honor life's journeys through the power and beauty of circle. As Manitonquat, a noted circle teacher, observes in *The Circle Way*, "When we are in a circle again, it feels like coming home."

The Power of Circle

In circle we share stories that reflect both our common and unique experiences. Through these stories we find our voice and make visible what is important to us. Circle allows us to shift our perspective, giving us new and useful ways of seeing ourselves and the world around us.

The power of circle comes from the acknowledgment and inclusion of each person present. Everyone is accepted for what they bring to circle. Simply arranging chairs or pillows in a circle so everyone can see each other supports a sense of being a valued part of the group. To slow the pace of conversation and ensure that everyone has an opportunity to speak in circle, a special item may be chosen and used as a talking piece. As it passes around the circle, each person holding it has an opportunity to speak uninterrupted while others listen.

When we gather in a group, too often conversations cross over and, rather than listening, we interrupt each other to express what is on our minds. In circle, however, we create a space for us to truly listen to one another. As Margaret Wheatley observes in her book, *Turning to One Another,* "I think the greatest danger to good conversation is that we've lost the capacity to listen. We're too busy, too certain, too stressed. We don't have time to listen." In a fast paced and highly mobile society, circle offers us a time out and a space for reflection and celebration.

Ceremony can be an important and powerful part of circle if appropriate for your setting and those present. It announces that an event or space is to be honored. Ceremony helps us transition from our busy lives into a different space where we can be fully present. It can be as simple as lighting a candle in the center of the circle. Each of us may be asked to bring an item that holds special meaning to share its significance and place in the center of the circle. This is a visual reminder of the gifts each of us brings to the circle. In *Calling the Circle*, author and teacher, Christina Baldwin, writes that the center of the circle represents the collective energy of the group. These simple acts of ceremony help us celebrate every-day life and important milestones in our lives.

Circle gatherings embrace all people, thoughts and beliefs. We can be ourselves, have a voice, and be received in a nonjudgmental and caring way. Circle is a place where we can speak from our hearts about what is important in our lives. By sharing what has meaning to us, we begin to know others and ourselves in new ways. We create connection and community by sharing the mysteries and joys of our lives.

Circle Stories

In the following stories you hear the voices of people who have been in circle as they reflect on their experiences and how circle has affected their lives. These stories give insight to the many ways circles can be used and provide ideas for planning and holding a circle.

The Circle and the Rock

Catherine's Story

The rock appeared halfway through the summer writing workshop I was teaching last July. When I opened the classroom one day, it was lying on the table - a plain, gray rock the size of a saucer and about an inch thick. The edges were rounded - proof of its origin: a beach on the North Shore of Lake Superior. I never knew how it got into our room, but the rock stayed on the table for the rest of the class as we wrestled with how to write personal essays.

At the end of the week, the rock appeared at the class farewell party and literally made the rounds. One round, anyway: it was the talisman that each class member held while speaking "in circle" that night. I had participated in a couple of casual circles before - one group of friends does this twice a year, lighting a candle and making a wish, then listening as each person in the group repeats the wish. It's a comforting ritual, but it hadn't prepared me for what happened at this circle.

One by one, each of the 16 students - all adults, nearly all women - held the flat, gray stone and talked about what the week had meant personally. I no longer remember the sequence, and that surprises me - it's only been two months. But I remember what happened and how I felt, and that's all that counts.

Several people wept and, halfway around, so did I. They were all saying thanks - thanks to each other for sharing and support, thanks to the program that sponsored the class, and thanks, finally, to me. My self-confidence, I should admit at this point, is only skin-deep. I often struggle to keep my spirits up, am quick to put myself down and have trouble remembering or believing praise. But in this circle, as the flat rock moved from hand to hand, that was what I was getting: praise, praise and more praise.

I listened, at first in amazed disbelief, then in growing joy, as my students - now my friends - told me what a good teacher I was. "You are the definition of a teacher," one woman said. "I am a different person - I've changed," said another.

All the while, I listened to two voices - the speaker's and my own inner one. Mine, for a change, was saying, "Believe it! Believe it. This time, really believe it! These are people you respect, and all sixteen of them can't be wrong. They're credible people. Believe them! Believe them!"

And to my amazement, I have.

It took 16 people and a chunk of Lake Superior rock to pound it into me, but this time I really did believe their praise. I still do. A 16-person circle is just too hard to argue with. My self-critical side has finally had to bite its tongue. And in that sweet silence, I am enjoying the most productive Fall - personally and professionally - that I can remember! I am truly grateful - to the group, to Sherry who suggested and led the circle, and to the mystery person who brought the rock.

The rock, by the way, went home with me. It's on my night stand now, where I can touch it evenings and mornings - and remember."

The Talking Piece

The following story was written by a participant of Catherine's circle held at the end of the week-long writing class to honor her. With just one round of the talking piece for each person to reflect on their week together, Sharon recalled her thoughts as the talking piece made its journey around the room and it became her turn to speak.

Sharon's Story

16 women and one man, seated in a circle around the living room. The light is dim, the night comfortably cool. Light chatter ripples and pops around the room, an aura of expectant energy permeates the atmosphere.

The circle begins with the honoring of our teacher Catherine. The talking piece is passed to the left, beginning its journey around the circle. As the stories begin, I listen and appreciate each one. When the talking piece nears me, a joyous anticipation, as well as that momentary sweaty-palm, heart-thump that comes before speaking in public, fills me. My eagerness to share rises, yet I am fully immersed in what others are saying – I can feel what they speak to. I take the stone talking piece in my hand. Heavy and warm, it radiates the energy of all who had so far told their stories, connecting us to each other. I feel my energy enter and warm the talking piece. While speaking my words, it seems as only Catherine and I exist – then the rest of the room comes back – strong, vibrant, connected, like a loving web holding goodwill.

The talking piece is passed along, hand to hand, and I watch everyone speak to Catherine. When they finish, each person looks at me and everyone else in communion. I feel my energy attached to them through the talking piece, through the atmosphere of laughter, smiles, a few tears. How wonderful to be able to tell someone openly how special they are in our usual stoic world - mine is not so stoic, but I am reserved about sharing feeling with people, as many are uncomfortable with being told how special they are and how they touch us.

How to describe this feeling of being in circle and expressing our thoughts? When we honor another it brings the best we have to the forefront, a lightness of spirit. It is added to what others offer in the circle, building connection and trust.

Emily's 21st Birthday

Nancy's Story

Planning a circle to celebrate my daughter's 21st birthday was a perfect way to bring people together to celebrate this milestone in her life. Before the circle, invited friends and family were asked to think about their experiences of turning 21 and to bring these stories, along with their hopes for Emily, to share at the birthday circle. They were also asked to bring an item or a reading symbolizing the meaning of a transition in their lives.

The circle was held in the living room of a friend. Furniture was arranged in a circle with a round table in the middle. Seven people were present and two friends, unable to attend, sent messages to be read. To help create the center, Emily was given a gift box containing a small cloth, a large candle and nine small candles - one for each person. She placed these items in the center of the table.

We welcomed everyone by saying, "Thank you for coming and being a part of this celebration. We are here to honor a special time in Emily's life. In honor of the light you bring here today, we would like each of you to light a candle." As we went around the circle, everyone introduced her/himself and lit a candle; two candles were also lit for those unable to attend. Her father and I then read favorite verses from *Poem in October* by Dylan Thomas and *Little Gidding* by T.S. Eliot.

During the second round, each person shared what she/he had brought that symbolized turning 21 and told personal stories about transitions in their own lives. These stories highlighted the ongoing changes and possibilities that are presented to us throughout our lives. Messages from a favorite high school teacher and a family friend were also read. One person, nearing retirement, shared a story about the excitement of pursuing new interests and challenges. As we completed the circle a final time, everyone shared their hopes for Emily and extinguished her/his candle.

Emily then gave each person an agate from the north shore of Lake Superior. The rings of the agate were a metaphor for the many layers of life. Everyone was thanked for coming and a reading closed the circle. After the circle we enjoyed dinner and cake together.

The stories that were shared deepened my understanding and appreciation for each person. It was a special way to celebrate an important transition in my daughter's life.

Jon's Story (Emily's father)

This was my first experience participating in a circle. Although the process of circle was explained to me before Emily's gathering, I felt a little unsure about exactly how I would fit into the circle. I knew I would give a short reading, and I found it comforting to know I had a specific role, that my participation wasn't going to be completely ad lib.

Once the circle got going I was pleasantly surprised to find that it was easy and natural to participate, that the format and culture of the circle promoted participation by all. The circle was split age-wise between people in their early 20's and people 55 and over. I thought this difference in ages might cause communication problems or a clash of perspectives, but I was pleased to observe just the opposite.

Any apprehensions I had before participating in my first circle vanished shortly after the circle began. I found the experience enjoyable and enlightening and look forward to participating in another circle. Each participant brought a unique perspective, wisdom and insight and humor that, when combined with everybody else, created an unexpectedly rich and enjoyable whole.

Emily's Story

My birthday circle was great fun and very special. Usually birthday celebrations are a big party where the "birthday person" opens gifts and has cake. This kind of birthday celebration can sometimes feel impersonal. My birthday circle made it easy for each person, whatever their age, to share their wisdom and excitement about pursuing new interests and challenges. This circle with my family and friends made my 21st birthday especially memorable.

Lorraine's 85th Birthday

Lorraine's Story

It was a beautiful July weekend, sunny and warm. The lake home had been opened to us to celebrate my 85th birthday. Family had come from Oregon, Utah and Minnesota for a reunion. There were fifty-two of us from four generations. A happy time of games, water fun, pontoon rides and picnics. The final evening was reserved to honor my birthday.

I can still see it now - there was a table set in the middle of the patio. It was covered with one of my many afghans. Fifty-two chairs and benches were placed in a large circle and everyone was called to take a seat. I know there was a look of awe, anticipation and wonder on my face as all came to gather into the circle. The little ceremony began with the traditional "Happy Birthday" song. Then, one by one, each one rose to tell his or her own Grandma story and express love, respect and gratitude to me. The first to rise was a grandson-in-law who told of his first meeting with me fifteen years earlier.

And so it went 'round the circle, each with his or her own feelings and experiences for this family matriarch. Two beloved grandsons sat in front of me playing their guitars and singing in harmony, "I Can't Help Falling in Love With You." The last to rise was the youngest son who had opened their home to the family. Tears streamed down my cheeks as I tried to express my gratitude and affection for each one of them. This circle of love is burned deep into my heart and soul for the rest of my days.

Once in a Blue Moon

Eileen's Story

This circle was meant to be. It all seemed so right - no apprehension. I asked my friend Jodi to host the circle with me - what a fun time it was for us! We were like two girls planning a very special party. It was easy - it did not seem like work. We divided up what needed to be done and it all fell into place. My objective was to have a group of women gather to enjoy an evening of friendship and to experience something new. It was a new experience for me as well.

We had a great mix of women - a total of thirteen who truly wanted to come and experience this circle. The night before, I arranged the room, lit candles, sat down, listened to music and tried to imagine what the next night would be like. The room felt so warm and inviting for me. I hoped the same for those who were coming.

When Jodi came with her decorations the night of the circle, it all came together so beautifully. Candles, a feminine statue, items from nature and special beadwork pieces I created for each participant were placed on fabric in the center of the circle - it was a room transformed into an inviting, mystical space.

When the women arrived and we began, I didn't feel nervous - just anxious and excited for the night to finally be here. It felt so neat to gather a group of women together that was so diverse and yet had so much in common. I enjoyed feeling their energy and watching how the evening flowed. The warm, comforting, respectful setting allowed people to open up and trust. It gave them a chance to recharge their soul.

Highlights of the circle for me were inviting family and friends, creating a warm and inviting space, preparing the center of the circle, making the special beadwork pieces and putting a lot of thought into creating a really unique experience. We came up with four questions that were a good mix for circle rounds: Share something you feel is a blessing or brings happiness in your life; Share how you have been affected by the energy or cycles of the moon; Share a turning point or important transition in your life and how it changed you; and Share with us a woman (living or deceased) who you admire or honor and why. They were non-threatening but made us dig deep if we wanted to. The last round of the talking piece was really special. We asked everyone to express whatever they would like -

they could add to whatever had been talked about in circle or bring up something new. We had no idea how this would play out. It was great, watching the circle take on a life of its own.

As the evening came to a close, my heart was so full. I was so blessed to experience this with an awesome group of women. I did not want it to end. Our "Once in a Blue Moon Celebration Circle" far exceeded anything I could have imagined or hoped for.

Summer Solstice Celebration

Sandi and Sherry's Story

Our day and a half Solstice Celebration was planned and hosted by us at our neighboring cabins. Our purpose was to create a fun and meaningful gathering for a group of eight friends, most of who had never experienced a circle and were a little apprehensive about coming. We were asking friends to come to a new "place" with us, a place we hadn't yet shared in our relationship. Hosting a circle for this particular purpose was new to us too.

Our intention for gathering in circle was to honor self and celebrate the Summer Solstice. Guests were invited to bring a salad and a small valued item to share its story and place in the center of the circle.

We offered reflexology, massage, a special activity and free time for relaxation. The activity we chose was collecting stones from the shore and gluing them to a wood frame that each person would use for a group picture.

Everyone's fears about participating in something new dissipated once circle started. We opened with an inspirational reading and a candle dedication. We followed with honoring the longest day of the summer by reflecting on the light, warmth and energy the sun brings to our lives.

For the first round of the circle we introduced ourselves and shared a recent blessing, using a rose quartz heart as a talking piece. The second round brought touching stories as participants shared the items they had been asked to bring for the center of circle: an antique snow globe from a grandfather, a family picture and a book of prayers were among the things that brought laughter, joy and tears as their meaning was shared.

For a circle activity, each person received a sheet of paper with the following thought-provoking questions: What makes me laugh?, What is my passion?, What gives me confidence?, What am I most grateful for?, What is my greatest gift? and What one person has been the most influential in my life and why? There was time to reflect on the questions before sharing our responses in circle. We closed the morning circle with an inspirational reading.

In the afternoon, we gathered stones along the shore for our picture frames; we were children once again, curiously searching for treasure. Lying in the hammock became a respite for some while others read or kayaked between their body massage and reflexology therapy.

For dinner we donned bibs and sat at a table covered with newspaper to receive a surprise meal Sandi prepared for us. "Dump Dinner," a huge kettle of shrimp, sausage, corn on the cob and vegetables was spread before us, becoming delicious finger food!

We spent the evening relaxing and visiting and our friends stayed overnight in our cabins. The following morning we decorated our frames with our stones from the shore and a neighbor took a group picture. Lunch followed and we gathered back in circle. We did the Appreciation Activity (in the Appendix) highlighting how each of us is valued within our circle of friends. In a final passing of the talking piece, we retrieved our items from center as we shared thoughts on our time together. We closed by reading a poem together.

Linda, a first time circle participant commented, "I felt I had been part of a deepened connection with people whom, for the most part, I already had a very deep connection. It reinforced that there is always more available to learn about, and appreciate, in others."

9/11

Sherry's Story

At the time we began our book, our nation had just experienced the bombing of the Trade Center in New York City on September 11th, 2001. Shock was followed by a deep concern about how to respond to this tragedy. As a country, we experienced a major shift in perspective concerning our safety and freedom. Bioterrorism became a new awareness with the spread of the anthrax virus and other possible threats. We heard the words that "Nothing will ever be the same in our country again" and we watched as changes were happening to reflect that. Added security, loss of jobs, a downturn in the economy, a heightened awareness and quest for global news were some of the outcomes.

With the loss of so many lives, 9/11 became a catalyst for reassessing our priorities. We began to refocus on what holds true meaning in our lives. There was a deep sadness over what had happened but there were also redeeming characteristics evolving. A group of us decided to come together in circle to share our thoughts and honor our responses to this tragic event.

We sent out invitations entitled, "An Evening of Reflection and Celebration" to center around the "recent events in our nation and honoring our responses to them." We gathered in my home for potluck followed by circle. Participants were asked to bring a candle with a base to place in center and a dish to share.

My thoughts focused on how to prepare the space and set the tone for our gathering. A miniature crystal globe felt appropriate for a talking piece. We gathered pillows from around the house to sit on and moved furniture to support a circular arrangement of sitting. A plant and a "circle of friends" candle were placed on a cloth in the middle of the circle. Two smaller candles were placed there also, representing two women who could not attend. Music helped set the tone for the arrival of guests.

Seven people responded to the invitation. As they arrived, each person placed their candle on the perimeter of the circle where they would be sitting. We shared conversation and laughter while eating around the dining room table, setting the tone for the circle to come. Once gathered in circle, we shared a breathing and movement exercise to help us become relaxed and focused.

A participant offered to light a "circle of friends" candle and to make a dedication in honor of a loved one whom she had recently cared for until her death. We then lit the candles honoring the women who were unable to attend.

We talked about what circle is, what it represents and our purpose for gathering. The words of Qigong instructor Chunyi Lin were shared: "The September 11th tragedy was a catalyst. There has been an energy shift that we cannot stop but we can soothe it. As individuals we need more practice to deal with this energy. We need to help balance energy in the world. If we give out anger and frustration, we will create more of that. If we give out compassion and love we will create more of that. This event is asking us to respond in a different way." We responded in a different way by coming together in circle to acknowledge our part in creating peace and healing for self, the community and the world.

After introducing the talking piece, we began the first round. Participants introduced themselves and shared a recent blessing. The second round focused on how the tragedy changed our life and how it made us look at the world differently. As each of us spoke, we lit our candles. The third round focused on what we can do personally to promote peace and healing. During the last round we retrieved our candles from the center, blew them out and commented on our evening together.

We closed with a reading from the book, *A Grateful Heart: Daily Blessings for the Evening Meal from Buddha to the Beatles,* edited by M.J. Ryan. This reading was adapted from *The Week of Prayer for World Peace, 1978.*

> We pray for the power to be gentle: the strength to be forgiving; the patience to be understanding; and the endurance to accept consequences to holding what we believe to be right. May we put our trust in the power of good to overcome evil and the power of love to overcome hatred. We pray for the vision to see and the faith to believe in a world emancipated from violence, a new world where fear shall no longer lead men to commit injustice, nor selfishness make them bring suffering to others. Help us devote our whole life and thought and energy to the task of making peace, praying always for the inspiration and the power to fulfill the destiny for which we were created.

Bonnie, a circle participant, reflected her thoughts about having the opportunity to share her stories in circle: "I was in a safe place where I could express myself without reproach. In this circle, some told of their own fear, others of how 9/11 had not changed their day-to-day life. This circle provided an intimate setting to exchange our thoughts about the tragedy on September 11th and how it impacted us."

A Guide for Planning a Circle

Why create a circle gathering?
- honor a special person in your life.
- celebrate an event, milestone or shared interest.
- honor a group of people.

Who and how many should you invite?
- who shares an interest in the circle you have chosen?
- six to fifteen is a comfortable number for circle but we have also been in circles with more than twenty five.
- consider your space and what size group it will accommodate.

How long should a circle last?
- people are most receptive to a one to two hour time frame.
- add additional time if including an activity and/or meal.

How can you involve those coming?
- who would like to help plan the circle, bring an opening, a closing or a talking piece?
- what item/s related to the focus of the circle can others bring to share and place in the center?
- if planning a meal, will you ask others to bring a dish to share?

How do you invite others to your circle?
Invitations can be verbal, by e-mail or written and include:
- purpose for gathering
- what participants are to bring
- location, when it begins and ends, directions
- phone number for contacts and RSVP

What kind of space do you want to create?
- what will help create the space you want: different lighting, music or decorations?
- how much ceremony do you want to include?

Do you want to create a center for the circle?
- is creating a visual center, with a special cloth, candle/s or items related to the focus of the circle, appropriate for your group?
- what will you place in center before the gathering?
- what will you ask others to bring to place in the center?

Who will choose and bring the talking piece?
- who would like to bring the talking piece?
- what small item would reflect your purpose for gathering?

Who will choose and share an opening?
- what is an appropriate opening to help set the tone for your circle?
- who can you ask to give an opening?

Which questions will be used for the circle rounds?
- what questions fit the purpose of your circle?
- what questions help people connect and share stories?
- how many circle rounds will you have time for? In each round, plan for approximately 3 minutes per person.

Are there activities you want to include?
- add extra time if planning activities. If you want to share results of the activity in a circle round, allow extra time.
- if an activity is included, consider age appropriateness, the time available and the purpose of your circle.

Who will choose and share the closing?
- what kind of closing captures the essence of the circle you are holding?
- who can be invited to choose and present it?

Do you want to document or record the circle?
- recording your circle may keep people from fully participating. However, circles for birthdays, reunions or anniversaries may create memories and stories the group may want to record.
- if you choose to record any part of the circle, first check with participants for permission.
- what type of recording will serve you/the group best - photos, journal, audio, video?

A Guide for Holding a Circle

What kind of space do you want to create for your circle gathering?
- consider background music or other ways to enhance the setting and purpose.
- arrange comfortable seating with chairs or pillows on the floor.
- if creating a visual center of the circle, place items there before others arrive.
- before the circle begins, turn off phones and message recorders.

How will you start the circle?
- thank everyone for coming.
- share the reason for gathering.
- remind people to turn off phones. If needed, share information such as location of bathrooms.
- share approximate time planned for circle and ask if anyone has to leave early.

How will you open the circle?
- you might, for example, light a candle and make a dedication to a person being honored or the event being celebrated.
- introduce the person presenting the opening and invite her/him to share the reason for choosing it.
- see suggestions for openings under individual circles in *Circle Themes*.

What group agreements are needed or appropriate?
- an agreement such as "What is said in circle stays in circle" helps keep the space respectful.
- other group agreements are listed in Notes on Holding a Circle in the *Appendix*.

How is the talking piece introduced?
- introduce the person who brought the talking piece and ask her/him to share its significance.
- share how the talking piece is used: only the person holding it speaks, when a person receives the talking piece, she/he may choose to pass; it is generally passed to the left. For additional suggestions, see Notes on Holding a Circle in the *Appendix*.

What is a circle round and how do you begin?
- begin with introductions and ask a question for participants to respond to such as, "Share a recent blessing," or "Share how you know the person being honored."
- each person shares the story of any items brought for the center.
- continue with questions chosen for circle rounds.
- if activities are included, they can be done individually or in a group and then shared in circle.

Closing Circle:
- introduce the person presenting the opening and invite her/him to share the reason for choosing it.
- see suggestions for openings under individual circles in *Circle Themes*.

Circle Themes

There are six circle themes in this section: Connections, Beginnings, Discovery, Transitions, The Journey, and The World Around Us and 48 circles which are grouped under these themes. In each of the circles we offer suggestions to help you in your planning. Choose from these or let them serve as an inspiration to create your own circle.

A related circle story, written from the perspective of a circle participant, begins each theme section. We also include an author's note, highlighting circle concepts.

Circles are used in a variety of settings, for many different occasions and can include people of any age and stage of life. The circle gatherings we created are generally one-time gatherings but could evolve into several circles held over a period of time. Let your imagination be your guide and explore what draws you and others to holding a circle!

How to use this section:

- Each circle contains six headings: Creating a Center, Choosing a Talking Piece, Opening the Circle, Questions for Circle Rounds, Activities, and Closing the Circle. There are several suggestions under each heading. Circles are flexible – feel free to mix and match ideas.
- For circle rounds, choose two or three questions for a one to two hour circle with 8 – 12 people. Consider having one to two questions in reserve in the event you have additional time.
- You may want to create your own circle title. For example, friends used our ideas from the circle "Celebrating Nature" and created two different circles, "A Spring Celebration Circle" and "Once in a Blue Moon."
- Questions for Circle Rounds can also be used for informal gatherings. For example, when with a group of friends, you may take turns sharing a favorite memory of your friendship.
- If you have control tendencies, try to relax and be open to silence and surprises.
- Keep in mind you want to create a respectful space for sharing, listening, and appreciating the stories and gifts of others.

The need to be heard turns out to be one of the most powerful forces in human nature. Being listened to means that we are taken seriously, that our ideas and feelings are known, and ultimately that what we have to say matters. *The Lost Art of Listening*.

– by Michael P. Nichols, Ph.D.

Circle creates a learning environment where each participant, in the telling of stories, becomes our teacher. As we hear others speak and we are listened to, we learn new ways to look at life and deepen our understanding of each other. *Celebration Circles*.

– by McCreight and Winter

You don't have to do anything fancy to use the circle process. . . just get together with some friends or associates and take turns speaking from the heart as best you can; use a stapler as a talking piece if that is what's handy. The important thing is to just do it. You will be amazed at how powerful it is.

– from www.co-intelligence.org/P-listeningcircles.html

Bring Together

Listen   Empathize

Bridge   Communicate

Link   **Connections**   Network

Exchange   Collaborate

Web   Flow

Understanding

Reminiscing Circle Story

Marcia's Story

An assisted living setting provides a variety of opportunities for using circle. One of the most meaningful activities at an assisted living home in our community has been a "Reminiscing Circle." Residents come to the gathering bringing an item of special meaning to share with others. Perhaps it is linked to a precious memory or a particular challenge, or it may symbolize a certain phase or purpose in their life story. Thus the circle creates its own theme and talking pieces.

As the individual shares her/his story about the item, invariably others recollect memories of their own. We listen to each participant's unique story and then, as the item is passed, invite others to add the stories it triggers for them.

Favorite "Reminiscing Circle" items at the assisted living home have included art work, wedding and military photos, handmade items created by ancestors, symbols of faith and a beautiful braided lock of hair quietly treasured for seventy years. The outcome is usually wonderful and always unpredictable. An old set of dish towels, made from white flour sacks and hand embroidered with the days of the week, were familiar to everyone. Caressing or holding an old-time dishtowel to their cheek brought back memories of family meals, cozy kitchens with wood crackling in the stove. There were memories regarding chores and responsibilities, of laundry days so cold the towels were frozen solid the instant they were hung on the clothesline.

One resident shared an old confirmation book and a pastor's tender letter of affirmation that was an encouragement to her as a young girl - his letter affirmed qualities he saw in her. These qualities are still visible now, in the woman of 87, and are the very strengths that have carried her through a diverse and challenging life.

In one circle a woman reminisced about a long, golden tress of braided hair cut some seventy years ago. She is a woman of quiet demeanor, whose hearing is poor, whose sight is minimal and whose lovely hair is the same golden color. Woven into her story is a glimpse of a young woman with an artist's spirit and the heart of a musician. The circle also brought into focus losses she has faced: home, spouse, sight, hearing, dancing ... no, maybe not dancing, as the assisted living home recently had guest musicians and, as they played, residents danced and they were ageless.

Life stories unfold with strong emotion and a panorama of experiences including laughter and loss, glory and grief, dancing and disappointment. A truly good story cannot be told without feelings and, honoring them as they emerge, is one of the great gifts of circle.

Participants need time for reflection and closure when circle is coming to an end and closing in a positive tone is especially important when reminiscing. The spirit of circle lifts up participants and validate their stories. If painful memories surface, participants are encouraged to identify what makes the memory precious and what gifts it gives to them. Closure is a great time to reflect back over the circle and pick up threads of humor. A poem, story or funny thought-provoking saying can also be part of concluding the circle. Hugs are appropriate.

Circle is a place to share life's lessons and the essential wisdom of both "holding on and "letting go." Circle creates community where stories are valued and the storytellers are validated.

Author's Note

Each item brought by a participant in this circle became a talking piece. The items were passed from person to person to evoke memories by those holding them. This created more opportunities for participants to share than if a single talking piece had been used.

When asked to select one special item to bring to circle, it may take some thought and reflection or we may be drawn to something spontaneously. Questions often arise in one's mind when choosing the item: "What is important to me, what is something I value?" "What will I be comfortable sharing?" Having something physical to hold and talk about is a comfortable way to participate in circle. The space we create together becomes a safe place to share what holds meaning to us.

As participants of the Reminiscence Circle told their stories surrounding the item they brought, life was affirmed and what they value was brought to mind and treasured once again. Because this is an on-going circle, the group creates a rich community they can count on for continued sharing.

Table Talk

Think of the times you have gathered around the table to visit with friends, family, or associates. Too often our conversations cross over and we seldom get to hear what everyone is saying. Brief gatherings, even over lunch, are an opportunity for sharing stories. Ask if everyone would like to go around the table taking turns responding to a question about a shared interest, experience or current topic. Ask for suggestions and agree on one or two questions. Remind people that they have a right to pass when their turn comes.

This is the simplest of circles as it can be done with little preparation. You do not need to place anything in the "center" and if you ask the group to listen respectfully as each person speaks, you may choose not to use a talking piece.

Family gatherings, a meal with friends or associates, or a celebration such as a birthday are opportunities for a spontaneous circle. Wherever a small group of people gathers is a great place for circle if they are open to sharing stories.

The following are ideas for questions to use in a circle round. You may also check individual circles for other ideas:

- if you could have lunch/dinner anywhere in the world, where would it be and who would it be with?
- what is one thing you have always wanted to do?
- is there a book or movie that has had a special impact on you?
- whom do you admire or who is a role model for you?
- what inspires you?
- what is one thing you would like to know more about?
- what in nature do you most enjoy?
- what is a favorite childhood memory?
- is there a special place you enjoy being and what draws you there?
- what does aging mean for you?

Family Night

Our lives are increasingly complex with more and more activities competing for our time. This busyness can lead to feeling disconnected from those important to us. Participating in a circle enriches the times when we are together by setting aside a time and space for us to listen to each other. It helps us pay attention to what deepens and sustains the relationships we value.

The Family Night Circle can be a single circle or planned on a regular basis to bring people together to share favorite memories, interests, and how to support each other. A family circle is also a way for stepfamilies or blended families to strengthen connections by learning about each other's interests, values, and goals. This circle could be adapted for a gathering of sisters and/or brothers.

The circle could be informal, held around the dinner table, or more thoroughly planned and held before or after a meal. If the circle meets on a regular basis, involve others by rotating who chooses the talking piece and offers the opening and closing. Having each family member share in creating the meal is a fun way to engage everyone, or if there are several families involved, a potluck is a nice addition to this circle.

Under each of the following headings, there are several suggestions listed. Choose which are appropriate for your gathering; consider those participating and the time you have available.

Creating a Center:
The host and/or participants may provide the following items. Place these items in the center before the circle and/or during a circle round.
- something that represents a favorite activity, book, talent, trip, food, holiday or memory
- an item symbolic of what you value about your family
- a small item that brings happiness to your life
- favorite photographs
- items that hold special meaning for you or the family

Choosing a Talking Piece:
- a valued item such as book or toy
- something that represents a favorite activity, game or place to visit
- an item that symbolizes the importance of family
- a valued item passed down in the family

Opening the Circle:
- share a special story or memory of the family.
- read an excerpt from a journal, letter or family history.
- share an inspirational reading or special music.
- read a poem or portion of a favorite book (this could also be something written by a family member).

Questions for Circle Rounds:
- introduce yourself and share something you like about being a part of your family.
- share the story of any items brought for the center of the circle.
- share something you value about each other.
- what makes you happy?
- what is your favorite activity? What do you enjoy about it?
- what lessons and values guide your life?
- what would you like to do if you had the courage?
- what is your favorite childhood memory?
- share something you accomplished that you are proud of.
- relate a story about something positive you have learned from being a part of this family.
- what is your favorite holiday? Share why.
- share something you would like to learn more about.
- if you can take one thing or person to a deserted island to keep you company, what or who would it be?
- name a person in your life, living or no longer living, and the gifts you received from them.
- share a story about a challenge in life you overcame.
- what is the craziest thing you ever did or would like to do?
- what is your favorite toy/music/book/place/house?
- how do you play? How is it part of your life?
- how do you work? How is it part of your life?
- what prejudice do you dislike the most?
- relate a story about the value of family.
- what are your hopes for your family/families?

Activities:
- see Appreciation, A Gift Sharing, Celebration Wreath (make a family wreath with each person bringing an item representing a special memory), A Wall of Memories and Sharing Values listed under Activities in the *Appendix*.

Closing the Circle:
- each person shares an insight gained from the circle and her/his parting thoughts.
- see suggestions under Opening above.

Getting to Know You

Plan this circle for a group of people who want to learn more about each other or welcome someone new into a community. The setting could be a home, at school, in the community, or the workplace. A potluck meal before or after circle is a great addition to this circle as it gives everyone an opportunity to informally relax and get to know each other.

Under each of the following headings, there are several suggestions listed. Choose which are appropriate for your gathering; consider those participating and the time you have available.

Creating a Center:
The host and/or participants may provide the following items. Place these items in the center before the circle and/or during a circle round.
- a candle or flowers
- a book of information and resources about the community compiled by everyone present
- a written welcome from each person present
- items representing an interest of each person present
- a small item symbolic of what brings happiness to your life
- gifts (examples: a welcome mat or tickets to a local event)

Choosing a Talking Piece:
- a valued item brought by a participant
- an item reflecting an interest of the person or group
- a small book of good wishes

Opening the Circle:
- share a special welcome for the individual and/or group.
- make a candle dedication to welcome the new person into the community.
- share a reading about friendship or new beginnings.

Questions for Circle Rounds:
- introduce yourself and share how you know the person/s honored or how you came to live or work in your community.
- share the story of any items brought for the center of the circle.
- share what you like most about this neighborhood/community/place of work/school.
- share your favorite place for entertainment or eating.
- what is your favorite activity or sport?
- what do you like to do for relaxation?
- describe a skill you can share with your neighborhood/coworkers/class-mates?
- see other circles such as Family Night or Honoring Friendships.

Activities:
- see Art and Sharing Values listed under Activities in the *Appendix*.

Closing the Circle:
- read from a book of well wishes created by everyone present.
- present gifts - a book of well wishes, a welcome mat or any other gifts brought by participants.

Parent and Child

This circle explores and celebrates the relationship between a child and a parent or someone who is in a parental role. It is a way to connect and learn more about each other through the simple process of telling stories that hold special meaning. The circle might include a group of parents and their children or the focus could be on a single parent-child relationship and include extended family and friends. Involving grandparents for a three-generational circle adds wisdom and richness to the gathering.

In this circle special memories are shared and people highlight what they value about the parent-child relationship. The setting could be a home or cabin, around a campfire, during a tea or luncheon, or at a community building. This circle could also simply be one or two circle rounds with the talking piece after an outing.

Under each of the following headings, there are several suggestions listed. Choose which are appropriate for your gathering; consider those participating and the time you have available.

Creating a Center:
The host and/or participants may provide the following items. Place these items in the center before the circle and/or during a circle round.
- handmade quilt or favorite family table cloth
- a candle, garden flowers
- favorite photos
- favorite childhood items of each parent and child pair
- items passed down through the generations of each family present
- items reflecting shared interests or activities of each parent and child pair
- gifts to be presented

Choosing a Talking Piece:
- an heirloom
- a symbol or charm representing a parent and child
- something created or chosen by a parent and child
- an item symbolic of the parent's or child's generation (music, events, people, activities)
- something representing a shared interest, activity or trip

Opening the Circle:
- make a candle dedication honoring the parent and child relationship and what each brings to each other's lives.
- share a reading honoring the parent/child relationship.
- a grandparent, parent or child shares a story about a favorite activity, interest or memory.
- read a selection from books such as *The Quotable Mom*, Kate Rowinsky, Ed.

or *Thoughts to Share With a Wonderful Daughter (Mother or Son)* by Blue Mountain Arts.

Questions for Circle Rounds:
- introduce yourself and share a gift/blessing received from your parent or child.
- light a candle in honor of your relationship and place it in the center.
- share the story of items brought for the center of the circle.
- what is one of your favorite memories from childhood?
- share something you want your parent/child to know about you.
- share a favorite memory of each other.
- recall a funny moment about each other.
- tell a story about a shared activity or trip.
- share a story about receiving encouragement or support.
- share a time when you were a challenge to each other and how you overcame this.
- recall a time you learned something valuable from each other.
- share what you wish for each other.

Activities:
- see Art, Writing and Sharing Values listed under the Activities section in the *Appendix.*

Closing the Circle:
- each participant shares a wish for her/his parent/child.
- share a special reading or something written for the occasion.
- present gifts.
- refer to suggestions under Opening.

Mother's/Father's Day

A Mother or Father's Day Circle honors a parent (or someone who has been like a parent) by providing an opportunity to express appreciation for her/him in the presence of others. How often do we think of the gifts we have received from a parent but not taken the time to express what those gifts are and the importance they have in our lives? Gathering in a circle and using a talking piece invites this expression by providing a space for us to share stories honoring a parent.

This circle not only creates rich memories that a parent can enjoy, it is an opportunity to discover more about her/him. Consider including more than one generation. Plan the circle anytime of the year or on the traditional Mother's Day or Father's Day.

Ask the honoree/s if they would like to be part of planning the circle. They can help make up the guest list, provide the talking piece, read, or create a piece for an opening or closing. Children can have fun making presents or writing something special for the guest of honor. Each person can be invited to bring a favorite family dish to share for a potluck.

Hold this circle in a garden, a favorite room in a home, a clubhouse, or any environment that is special to the guest/s of honor. It could be part of an outing already planned for the honoree. As an example, when having dinner, ask one or two of the questions listed under Circle Rounds.

Under each of the following headings, there are several suggestions listed. Choose which are appropriate for your gathering; consider those participating and the time you have available.

Creating a Center:
The host and/or participants may provide the following items. Place these items in the center before the circle and/or during a circle round.
- photos of the different stages of the parent's life
- childhood items of the parent such as books, games, toys
- an heirloom
- items reflecting the parent's favorite activities, travel, art or sports
- gifts brought or created for the parent

Choosing a Talking Piece:
- an heirloom or spiritual symbol
- an item that reflects the parent's interests, values or accomplishments
- something of value chosen by the guest/s

Opening the Circle:
- share a story about the parent/s.
- read a favorite passage chosen by the parent/s.
- share a writing composed by the guest/s of honor or others.

Questions for Circle Rounds:
- introduce yourself and share a favorite memory about the guest/s of honor.
- share the story of any items brought for the center of the circle.
- share something you value about her/him.
- share something you have learned from the honoree/s and how it is important to you.
- what is one thing you would like the guest/s of honor to know about you?
- share a time you were a challenge for her/him and how the two of you overcame it.
- share a story about a trip/sport/activity you have done together.
- the parent/s share a story about each person present.

Activities:
- see Celebration Wreath, Candle Wishes and Wall of Memories listed under Activities in the *Appendix.*

Closing the Circle:
- each person shares a blessing for the honoree/s.
- the honoree/s or each person shares her/his closing thoughts.
- present gifts.
- refer to suggestions under Opening.

Grandparent's Day

Grandparents often hold a special place in the lives of their grandchildren. This intergenerational circle is a way to honor a grandmother and/or grandfather. The circle could take place any time during the year or on the Sunday in September designated to honor Grandparents. It could be held in a home, garden, family cabin, church, or community room.

Planning the circle with family members and including suggestions from the grandparent/s will make the gathering a rich experience. Share photographs and the stories surrounding them, lessons learned from the grandparents, special memories, or plan a combination of these. A potluck lunch or dinner with the family's favorite dishes will bring added enjoyment to the gathering.

Under each of the following headings, there are several suggestions listed. Choose which are appropriate for your gathering; consider those participating and the time you have available.

Creating a Center:

The host and/or participants may provide the following items. Place these items in the center before the circle and/or during a circle round.

- a special cloth/quilt created by a family member
- garden flowers
- a candle/s in a favorite color or scent of the grandparent/s
- items reminiscent of their lives
- items made by the grandparent/s
- family heirlooms
- photos
- a book of memories compiled by everyone present
- gifts (example: coupons for time to spend with grandparent/s or gift certificates)

Choosing a Talking Piece:

- a family heirloom
- an item created by a grandchild and/or grandparent
- something that represents a special interest of the grandparent/s
- a valued item brought by the grandparent/s

Opening the Circle:

- play music selected by the grandparent/s.
- read something selected or written by the grandparents or a family member.
- make a candle dedication to the grandparent/s for their lessons and gifts.

Questions for Circle Rounds:

- introduce yourself and share something you admire about the honoree/s.
- light your candle with a dedication to the grandparent/s and place it in the

center.
- share the story of photos or items brought for the center of the circle.
- share a favorite memory of your grandparent/s.
- tell a funny story about them.
- recall the gifts/blessings you have received from your grandparent/s.
- share something you have learned from them.
- share your wishes/blessings for them.
- as each person holds the talking piece, the grandparent/s shares a favorite memory of them.

Activities:
- see Celebration Wreath, Candle Wishes and Wall of Memories listed under Activities in the *Appendix*.

Closing the Circle:
- each person blows out her/his candle with closing thoughts.
- everyone gives their blessing for the grandparents.
- present gifts.

Honoring Friendships

This circle is for a group of people who want to celebrate their friendship. It is an opportunity to share stories about their shared journeys and learn more about each other. In circle we communicate at a deeper level than in our every day conversations. Our words reflect more of who we are and as the talking piece makes its rounds, we come to know each other in a different way.

As we tell our stories in circle, we come to appreciate more fully the meaning we hold in each other's lives. We also learn more about ourselves as others share how they have grown through their friendships with us. Gathering in circle to honor these special relationships highlights their importance in our lives and strengthens a sense of community and connection.

A group of friends that already share an activity such as quilting, a book club, or a special sport can create a circle easily as they are in communication on a regular basis. For those who do not see each other often, a friendship circle could become the way to meet once a year to reconnect.

The setting for a friendship circle could be at any place that friends usually gather. It could be part of a weekend retreat, a day outing, or simply an hour to two at a friends house. Consider using a question or two listed under headings, there are several suggestions listed. Choose which are appropriate for your Circle Rounds at an already established gathering.

Under each of the following gathering; consider those participating and the time you have available.

Creating a Center:
The host and/or participants may provide the following items. Place these items in the center before the circle and/or during a circle round.
- an item symbolic of what you value about your friends
- photographs of places or people special to you
- a favorite cloth/quilt
- candle/s
- flowers, items from nature
- something that represents a favorite activity
- written memories of shared journeys or what friendships mean to you

Choosing a Talking Piece:
- a symbol of friendship (example: friendship ring, a photograph)
- a small book about the meaning of friendships
- something that represents a favorite group activity or event

Opening the Circle:
- offer a deep breathing exercise or a guided meditation.
- give a group back rub; everyone stands, turns to the left and massages the person in front of them.

- make a candle dedication to the journeys shared through friendship.
- share a special story about the group of friends.
- share a passage, poem or music about the meaning of friendship.

Questions for Circle Rounds:
- introduce yourself and share a recent blessing from a friend.
- share the story of any items brought for the center of the circle.
- share thoughts on the meaning of friendship.
- share something you value about being part of this group of friends.
- light your candle in honor of a friend/s and what they have brought to your life (this may be done silently or shared in circle).
- describe a lesson or value that guides your life.
- share the qualities of a friend you admire.
- how do you play? What does it mean to your life?
- share a favorite activity and how it influences your life.
- what brings you joy?
- when do you feel most peaceful?
- share something you accomplished that you are proud of.
- share a story about a challenge in life you overcame.
- share something you have never done but would like to do.
- what is your favorite childhood memory?
- share something you would like to learn more about.
- what is one thing you would like the group to know about you?
- if you could be with one person on a deserted island, who would it be?

Activities:
- write thoughts on the meaning of friendship, then share with the group.
- see Appreciation, A Gift Sharing, Art, Writing and Sharing Values listed under Activities in the *Appendix.*

Closing the Circle:
- each participant shares parting thoughts.
- see suggestions under Opening above.

Celebrating A Holiday

What are some of your favorite memories surrounding a holiday as a child? What kinds of activities brought you enjoyment and made this special time of year more meaningful for you? Coming together in circle to celebrate a holiday gives us the opportunity to explore these questions as we hear stories that evoke memories of holidays past. The circle may also focus on how we celebrate today or how other cultures celebrate their holiday. Refer to the Culture and Tradition Circle for additional ideas if including holiday traditions from different cultures.

Traditional holidays are typically a time when family and friends gather for the purpose of commemorating an event like Hanukah or Christmas. Other circle celebrations might highlight the meaning of holidays such as Thanksgiving, Memorial Day or Martin Luther King Day.

What are some favorite foods you or your guests associate with the holiday? Include them if you have time to share a meal or snack. Are there activities that recapture memories of past holidays or that have become traditional for you or those participating in the circle? Do you want to create a new tradition? Perhaps holding a circle as part of your holiday gathering can become a yearly event. This circle might even follow a holiday cookie making/exchanging party or a volunteer effort within the community such as caroling.

Under each of the following headings, there are several suggestions listed. Choose which are appropriate for your gathering; consider those participating and the time you have available.

Creating a Center:

The host and/or participants may provide the following items. Place these items in the center before the circle and/or during a circle round.

- spiritual or cultural symbols
- candle/s
- holiday fabric or cloth
- holiday flowers, greenery, items from nature
- holiday cake, cookies, chocolates decorated to represent the specific holiday
- items or photos of holiday traditions or spiritual journeys
- writings that reflect the meaning of the holiday
- readings of what the holiday means and how it is celebrated in other cultures
- childhood gifts or recollections of them
- art work or dolls that reflect the colors, clothing and traditions of the holiday from your culture or others

Choosing a Talking Piece:

- a spiritual symbol
- an item representing the holiday you are celebrating
- a small book with a holiday story that can be read for the opening or closing

• a special holiday photograph

Opening the Circle:
- share a reading that tells the origin and history of the holiday you are celebrating.
- tell stories that capture the essence of the holiday season.
- read excerpts from spiritual books.
- play holiday music, chimes or bells.

Questions for Circle Rounds:
- introduce yourself and share one of your favorite traditions for this holiday.
- share the story of any items brought for the center of the circle and place in the center.
- light your candle and honor a person you associate with this holiday and share her/his meaning in your life.
- recall a favorite memory of this holiday as a child.
- what were your beliefs about this holiday as a child and how have they changed?
- where is your favorite place to be for this holiday?
- did you or your family have a traditional spiritual activity for this holiday? What was it?
- is there a tradition you would like to establish for the future?

Activities:
- see A Gift Sharing, Celebration Wreath and Wall of Memories listed under Activities in the *Appendix*.

Closing the Circle:
- blow out candles and share parting thoughts.
- sing a holiday song or play holiday music.
- see suggestions above under Opening.

Book Club

A book club is a community of people enjoying a mutual interest - the love of books. Being in a club is an opportunity to discuss books that expand our world and reflect life's challenges, mysteries, and triumphs. Book clubs vary depending on the type of books chosen, where and how often the participants meet, and if social events are part of the group's activities.

A Book Club Circle is a way for members to deepen relationships and learn what others value about being in the club. Plan a circle to share favorite books, characters and authors, and to discover what members value about reading books. If planning a meal, club members might bring food related to the theme or setting of a book they have particularly enjoyed. A youth group or school class might also plan this circle to celebrate a favorite book.

Under each of the following headings, there are several suggestions listed. Choose which are appropriate for your gathering; consider those participating and the time you have available.

Creating a Center:

The host and/or participants may provide the following items. Place these items in the center before the circle and/or during a circle round.
- favorite books
- photos from book club events
- figures or photos representing favorite authors, characters or stories

Choosing a Talking Piece:
- something representing an author, character or setting in a favorite book
- a book mark
- a favorite book of the group
- a special pen or writing tool

Opening the Circle:
- read a brief passage from a favorite book.
- share quotes from authors or characters in a book.
- read a selection that reflects the value or enjoyment of reading.

Questions for Circle Rounds:
- introduce yourself as a favorite character from a book.
- share the story of any item you brought for the center.
- share a childhood memory about books or being read to.
- what was your favorite book when you were a child?
- share a story about a favorite book, character or author and how it influenced you.
- what do books and/or reading bring to your life?
- describe a favorite place you like to read.

- if you could be any character from a book, who would you be?
- what author would you most like to talk with? What would you ask her/him?
- have you had an opportunity to talk with an author? What did you learn?
- what drew you to the book club? What do you most enjoy about it?
- have you ever thought of writing a book? About what topic?

Activities:
- invite everyone to come dressed as a favorite character or author.
- choose one book and ask club members to write alternative endings or describe characters they think are missing.
- write a group poem; each person contributes one word or phrase about what she/he gained from the circle.

Closing the Circle:
- share insights gained from the circle.
- see suggestions under Opening.

Class Reunion

Including a circle as part of a class reunion enriches the experience of coming together and helps everyone get reacquainted. Reunions are often held over a weekend so the circle could be held either the day before or the day of the reunion. Consider whether your circle should be a group of classmates with whom you are personally connected or if you want to include other class members as well. If you include a large number of classmates, form several circles, possibly around shared interests or activities, and enlist the help of others to host them.

A Class Reunion Circle is an opportunity to catch up on each other's lives by sharing stories that connect the past with the present. The circle gathering could be held in a private home or a public facility. Planning a catered or potluck meal or snack before or after the circle allows more time to get reacquainted.

Under each of the following headings, there are several suggestions listed. Choose which are appropriate for your gathering; consider those participating and the time you have available.

Creating a Center:

The host and/or participants may provide the following items. Place these items in the center before the circle and/or during a circle round.

- an item featuring the class color or motto
- candles to honor a mentor, teacher or classmate
- class flower (if the graduating class had selected one)
- the year book
- photographs: choose a focus such as your family, school days, what you are doing today or what you wish for yourself in the future
- items reminiscent of school day
- a collection of addresses and phone numbers

Choosing a Talking Piece:

- something symbolic of the graduating class (examples: a picture of the class, class ring, class flower, class verse)
- an item representing an important school memory, activity or event
- something participants value about their present life

Opening the Circle:

- play music that was popular when you were in school.
- share a special story or memory of school days given by a/each participant.
- make a candle dedication honoring the presence of each person.

Questions for Circle Rounds:

- introduce yourself and share where you live and how far you have traveled to attend.
- share the story of items and photographs brought for the center of the circle.

- light a candle and make a dedication to a special mentor, teacher or class-mate and place it in the center.
- recall a teacher or fellow student and the gifts received from her/him.
- share a special memory from your school days.
- what is the most meaningful thing you have done since you graduated?
- share one of your greatest lessons in life.
- what is your favorite food? book? place to visit? way to have fun?
- what do you want to be when you grow up?
- what is your greatest joy?

Activities:
- see A Gift Sharing and Wall of Memories listed under Activities in the *Appendix*.

Closing the Circle:
- exchange ways to keep in touch.
- each person shares her/his hopes for the future.
- read an inspirational poem together.
- share music or a dance that was popular during the school/graduation time period.
- share what you value or have enjoyed from the reunion.

Family Reunion

A reunion circle is an opportunity to reconnect and share family stories. Consider what activities are planned for the reunion and find a one to two hour time period to invite a small group to gather in circle. Circles can be organized by age, generations, interests, geographic regions, family branches, or any combination of these. Several circles could be planned during the reunion. This circle can easily be adapted for a reunion of friends.

If family members want to record any part of the circle, identify someone in the group who will do this, but first ask participants if they are comfortable sharing what is said beyond the circle. Prepare a sheet to make it easy to record comments and memories. Include information such as the date, who was present, and the location. These records can then be organized as part of the family history and shared with others.

Under each of the following headings, there are several suggestions listed. Choose which are appropriate for your gathering; consider those participating and the time you have available.

Creating a Center:
The host and/or participants may provide the following items. Place these items in the center before the circle and/or during a circle round.
- an item symbolic of a lesson or value learned from a family member
- items representing the spirit of this family or a family member
- something representing the universal importance of family
- an item that reflects a favorite family memory
- special family photos

Choosing a Talking Piece:
- a family heirloom
- something representing an individual's or family's history, accomplishments or values
- a special photo
- an item symbolic of an important place, event, or activity of an individual or family
- an item representing a favorite family trait such as musical or athletic ability or humor

Opening the Circle:
- share a reading from a favorite family book.
- read an excerpt from a family letter, journal or creative writing.
- play music significant to the family - possibly performed by family members.
- share a favorite family saying or prayer.
- share a reading that reflects the meaning of family.

Questions for Circle Rounds:
- introduce yourself and tell how you are a part of this family.
- share the story of items brought for the center of the circle.
- share memories of favorite games, food, vacations, holidays, activities or houses.
- what are your hopes for the family?
- recall an important lesson learned from a family member.
- share favorite memories from a specific time period or age.
- what are your craziest family memories?
- share favorite memories of a family member who has passed on.

Activities:
- create a family tree using branches and hang significant historical items on the branches - photograph and share copies with others.
- create a photo album or family story book.
- see A Gift Sharing and Wall of Memories under Activities in the *Appendix*.

Closing the Circle:
- each person shares a blessing they have received from being part of the family.
- see suggestions under Opening.

Neighborhood/Community

Most of us need connection, acceptance, and a sense of community. We may find this by belonging to a group with a shared purpose such as a community organization, special interest group, or a church. It may also come from living in a neighborhood that has created an identity by holding special events, working together on projects, or simply by sharing a geographic area.

A Neighborhood and Community Circle is a way to bring people together and make everyone more visible to each other. This circle could be held annually, along with a potluck, to strengthen connections among those in the neighborhood and to welcome new people into the community. See ideas under the Getting to Know You Circle.

Under each of the following headings, there are several suggestions listed. Choose which are appropriate for your gathering; consider those participating and the time you have available.

Creating a Center:

The host and/or participants may provide the following items. Place these items in the center before the circle and/or during a circle round.

- something that represents what you like or value about the group or neighborhood
- favorite photographs of people, activities and events in the neighborhood or community group
- a list or photographs of favorite places in the neighborhood (examples: play areas, entertainment, restaurants, stores, parks, a friend's house)

Choosing a Talking Piece:

- an item representing an event, a tradition, values, goals or accomplishments of the group or neighborhood
- something symbolic of the spirit or what you value about your neighborhood or community

Opening the Circle:

- share a reading or music that reflects group values, traditions, past events or activities.
- share a reading or music that captures the meaning of neighborhood or community.

Questions for Circle Rounds:

- introduce yourself and share the story of what brought you to this neighborhood or community group.
- share the story of any items brought for the center of the circle.
- what do you like most about living here or being a part of this community group?

- what do you see as the strengths of this neighborhood or community group?
- is there something you have learned or gained from being a part of this neighborhood or group?
- share a wish or vision for this area or group. How could we work together to accomplish this?

Activities:
- see Art (create a collage that represents the community or neighborhood) listed under Activities in the *Appendix.*

Closing the Circle:
- everyone shares her/his hopes for the neighborhood or community.
- see suggestions under Opening.

Potential

Sunrise   Change

Exploration   Opportunity

Spring   Babies

Beginnings

Endings   Seeds

Excitement   Risk

Unknown   Possibilities

Fresh Start

Connie's 50th Birthday Story

Connie's Story

Birthdays rarely affect me adversely. I am not a woman who lies about her age, but as I approached my 50th birthday, a sense of dread and sorrow engulfed me. I had believed since I was young that fifty was old. In my mind, 50 was wrinkles, dumpy, and out of touch. What I really feared in turning 50 was becoming a middle-aged frump.

I realized that this was a silly, negative approach to aging promoted by the images we see on television. I knew that I would only be one day older and that I needed to change my attitude. Still, when I thought about turning 50, I wanted my friends and family beside me. I wanted them when I learned that circles could be used to celebrate special events and I knew that I wanted to have a birthday circle.

My husband had experience in leading circles, so I asked him to plan my circle. He asked our friend Nancy to help him but in reality, the circle seemed to have a life of its own. A group of about ten friends and family members came. All of them were asked to bring objects that reminded them of me or represented a passage in their lives. My sister and brother-in-law brought things I had made for them. The objects were arranged in the center of the circle along with some candles, creating a sacred space for us to focus on. The talking piece went around the circle twice, the first for everyone to identify what they had brought and explain why they felt it represented me, the second for everyone to make a wish or say a prayer for me. The circle lasted about two hours.

I experienced in the circle a connection to the girl I once was and it gave me an assurance of my future. My friends and family supported me and affirmed my path. I was transported into my fifties feeling whole, happy and deeply loved. As I said in my circle, I think turning fifty is something everyone should do at least once in their life.

Stephen's Story (Connie's husband)

I felt the most important part of planning this circle was to communicate with the participants - especially those who had not been in circle before, to remove any apprehension about participating. I told them about how long the circle would last, how many times they would be speaking as they related their stories about Connie and answered any questions they had.

Circles provide something people are hungry to be a part of - something that is not a hierarchy - because our culture today is full of that. Circle recognizes a more normal way of being. The shape is a big part of it - a big wheel with no beginning and no end. The format makes it different. It is a place to express tenderness. Now I see everything in circles. No wonder early cultures came up with circle - it brings us more in touch with nature. The connectedness of people in circle - it is about as connected as I can get with people outside my family.

Author's Note:

In this circle, there was a diverse group of people in terms of ages, backgrounds, beliefs and experience with circle. Some people knew each other, others did not, and most had not attended a circle before. When someone is unfamiliar with circle and expresses apprehension about attending, take time to answer their questions and, if they are willing, offer to involve them in some way.

There may be a tendency to over plan a circle from a need for structure or anxiousness as to whether people will enjoy the gathering. Trust it will flow once it starts as that is the nature of circle. In the end, this was a circle rich with laughter and stories from friends and family.

Birth/Adoption

This circle celebrates and explores how our lives are enriched and changed when there is an addition to our family. A baby or child can bring great joy, new expectations, and changes in lifestyle. The parent-child relationship brings forth a range of intense feelings both loving and challenging. Gathering in a circle with family and friends is an opportunity to share our stories and traditions about birth and new beginnings. This can be a source of support and encouragement for the new parents. Hold this circle as part of a baby shower or on its own as a way to welcome a new baby or adopted child into the family.

Under each of the following headings, there are several suggestions listed. Choose which are appropriate for your gathering; consider those participating and the time you have available.

Creating a Center:

The host and/or participants may provide the following items. Place these items in the center before the circle and/or during a circle round.

- baby blanket/cap or favorite item of the child's
- child or family photographs
- favorite childhood items of the parents or child
- something passed down from generation to generation
- gifts for the newborn, child and/or parents
- items that capture the significance of the birth or adoption
- a candle/s to honor the parents or child

Choosing a Talking Piece:

- a favorite toy, book or other item from the parent's or grandparent's childhood
- a special gift for the child
- a baby ring that will be given as a gift

Opening the Circle:

- light a candle and make a dedication to the parents/child.
- share a story about the birth or childhood of the parents.
- relate a story about the newborn or child being adopted.
- read a favorite passage from a book or poem.
- share an inspirational reading or prayer.

Questions for Circle Rounds:

- introduce yourself and share how you know the parents.
- share the story of any items you brought for the center of the circle.
- tell a favorite story about the parent's birth or childhood.
- what are your hopes for the child?
- what does this birth or adoption mean to you?

- what strengths do you see in the parents that they will bring to parenthood?
- share a story about other births in the family.
- share a story about family traditions around births.
- share a favorite childhood memory.
- share your feelings about being a parent and how it has influenced your life.

Activities:
- see Celebration Wreath and Candle Wishes listed in the Activities section of the *Appendix*.

Closing the Circle:
- read a nursery rhyme, inspirational words or a poem.
- recall a family story about birth or new beginnings.
- share a story about a special item or photograph.
- share wishes for the child and/or parent.
- present gifts.
- each person shares parting thoughts.

Naming Ceremony

Naming Ceremony is a custom used by ancient, indigenous cultures to introduce and welcome a baby into the community. Today Naming Ceremonies are still taking place and are an alternative to a church Christening or Baptism. Nicole Celeban, who conducts these ceremonies in Australia, states they are "an opportunity for you to state in front of your family and friends the unconditional love and care, support and encouragement that you will continue to provide as a parent." The ceremony is often used by interfaith families, parents who do not have a church affiliation or those who want their children to decide for themselves which religion to follow as they mature. Search the web for "Naming Ceremony and Nicole Celeban" to access information.

Gathering in a circle creates a special, inclusive space for a Naming Ceremony. A family member, friend or someone ordained can officiate. Individual mentors or supporters can be chosen for the traditional godparent role. Each person in the Naming Ceremony is a witness to the commitments made by the parents or mentors. When introducing an older child into the family, "The focus of the ceremony could be a special welcome to the family and an expression of love rather than a formal naming," states the British Humanist Association - another resource on the web to check when planning a Naming Ceremony.

Consider when the following would be most meaningful to the family: lighting a candle, blessing the child, statements of commitment from the parents and mentors, readings, music and contributions from brothers, sisters or anyone present.

A Naming Ceremony can last as long as the family chooses but the typical time is about 20 – 30 minutes followed with a meal or snack. This celebration is usually held in the home or, if a large number of people are invited, a comfortable place within the community.

Under each of the following headings, there are several suggestions listed. Choose which are appropriate for your gathering; consider those participating and the time you have available.

Creating a Center:
The host and/or participants may provide the following items. Place these items in the center before the circle and/or during a circle round.
- a special cloth or quilt
- candle/s, flowers
- sea/salt water for blessing the child
- spiritual items significant to the family
- a book for writing a special message from each person present
- gifts

Choosing a Talking Piece:
- an heirloom
- a spiritual symbol
- a special photo
- an inspirational book
- a small gift for the child, wrapped or unwrapped

Opening the Circle:
- share a spiritual reading.
- light a candle and make a dedication to honor the child.
- share a blessing for the child.
- parents, mentors and/or godparents express their love and commitment to the child.

Questions for Circle Rounds:
- introduce yourself and share a story of how you know the family of the child.
- share the story of any items brought for the center of the circle.
- express your wishes for this child.
- share how you would like to support this child as she/he grows.

Activities:
- provide each person with a sheet of paper that has the child's name and the date on the top. Ask everyone to write something or draw a picture that will help the child remember this special day. Have colored pencils, crayons or any other art items needed to create the remembrance. This activity was offered by Pastor Janeva Stromberg at a Baby Naming Ceremony.
- see Candle Wishes in the Activities section of the *Appendix*.

Closing the Circle:
- introduce the child.
- bless the child.
- share in a song.
- dance in a circle around the child and parents.
- present the gifts.

Birthday

A Birthday Circle is a wonderful way for family, friends, or coworkers to celebrate and honor an individual on her/his birthday. As you plan, it may help to consider these questions: Is the birthday an important milestone such as turning 21 or 50? Has the person experienced or accomplished something significant in the past year that could be highlighted as part of a birthday celebration? What are her/his special interests? What happened during the year or on the day of the person's birth? What memories do you have of special birthdays? You may simply want to ask each guest to bring something that reminds them of the person being honored. These items will naturally inspire stories about the guest of honor.

Include the person being honored in the planning unless the circle celebration is a surprise. In the birthday circles we have hosted, the honoree has made out the guest list and in one birthday circle, the honoree made copies of a special reading for everyone to thank them for their gift of friendship. For examples of birthday circles, see "Emily's 21st Birthday" and "Lorraine's 85th Birthday" under *Circle Stories* and "Connie's 50th Birthday Story" at the beginning of this section.

Under each of the following headings, there are several suggestions listed. Choose which are appropriate for your gathering, consider those participating and the time you have available.

Creating a Center:
The host and/or participants may provide the following items. Place these items in the center before the circle and/or during a circle round.
- items representing the birthday person (examples: a favorite activity, trip, interest or accomplishment)
- her/his birth announcement
- flower or birthstone
- items from special milestones in her/his life
- something that represents an event that occurred during the birth year
- favorite childhood pictures
- an item that reflects something you value about the birthday person
- candle/s
- a birthday cake

Choosing a Talking Piece:
- an item representing an interest or accomplishment of the person being honored
- something of value chosen by the birthday person
- a special item from childhood
- a gift to give the birthday person

Opening the Circle:
- light a candle and make a dedication to the birthday person.

- share an inspirational selection.
- read a favorite story, poem or nursery rhyme chosen by the birthday person.
- read something written especially for the occasion.
- play special music.
- see ideas under Birth/Adoption.

Questions for Circle Rounds:
- introduce yourself and tell how you know the person being honored.
- share the story of any items brought for the center of the circle.
- what do you value about her/him?
- what has been her/his gift to you?
- what are her/his strengths?
- what is a valuable lesson you have learned from her/him?
- share a funny or favorite memory about her/him.
- what are your hopes for her/him?
- share a story about your favorite birthday tradition.

Activities:
- see the Celebration Wreath, Candle Wishes, A Gift Sharing and Art listed in the Activities section of the *Appendix*.

Closing the Circle:
- each person shares a wish or blessing for the birthday person.
- read a passage created for the occasion.
- play music selected by the birthday person.
- sing Happy Birthday and enjoy a birthday cake together.

Wedding Shower

A circle is a unique way to honor a bride or couple. The circle gathering could be planned prior to or shortly after the wedding. If held after the wedding, it offers the bride or couple an opportunity to thank friends and family for their support. It is also a time for everyone to share wedding stories. The setting may be a home, public facility, church, or workplace. Consult the bride or couple about their preferences for a setting and, if they choose, include them in other aspects of the planning such as making the guest list and choosing something meaningful for the talking piece.

Under each of the following headings, there are several suggestions listed. Choose which are appropriate for your gathering; consider those participating and the time you have available.

Creating a Center:

The host and/or participants may provide the following items. Place these items in the center before the circle and/or during a circle round.

- symbols of love
- a handmade item such as a quilt or picture frame
- favorite flowers
- candle/s to honor the bride or couple
- written wishes for the bride or couple
- pictures of the bride or couple and/or wedding pictures of their parents
- something old, something new, something borrowed, something blue
- gifts

Choosing a Talking Piece:

- a family heirloom
- something symbolic of a union, love or the journey ahead
- an item to be presented as a gift to the bride or couple
- something chosen by the bride or couple
- a small book of verse on love or relationships

Opening the Circle:

- light a candle and offer a dedication with a blessing for the bride or couple.
- share a reading created for the event by the bride, couple or other family and friends.
- ask the wedding couple share the story of how they met.
- play favorite music of the bride or couple.

Questions for Circle Rounds:

- introduce yourself and share how you know the guest/s of honor.
- share the story of any items brought for the center of the circle.
- relate a favorite or funny memory of the bride or couple.

- tell a story about a lesson you have learned through a relationship.
- share a blessing you have received through a relationship.
- share a story about the power of love.
- the bride or couple express their gratitude to each person present.

Activities:
- see Celebration Wreath, Candle Wishes and Art in the Activities section of the *Appendix.*

Closing the Circle:
- read a special passage selected or created by the bride or couple.
- each person shares her/his closing thoughts.
- the host gives a blessing.
- present gifts.

Wedding/Union

A circle gathering naturally creates a space for honoring a special couple as they begin a new phase in their lives. The focus of a Wedding Circle can vary. Consider the following: Is this a first marriage? Are children involved? Are several families being joined? Who needs to be included in the planning? Who will attend? Are there family issues that affect the planning? These questions will help determine the focus of the circle. A Wedding or Union Circle may be used as the entire ceremony or as part of the wedding day. If it is the entire ceremony, consider when to include an exchange of vows and rings.

Under each of the following headings, there are several suggestions listed. Choose which are appropriate for your gathering; consider those participating and the time you have available.

Creating a Center:
The host and/or participants may provide the following items. Place these items in the center before the circle and/or during a circle round.
- a special cloth, candle and flowers
- a collage of pictures of the couple from different times in their lives
- a candle brought by each person to light in honor of the couple
- written wishes or hopes for the couple
- items representing what will help guide the couple on their journey ahead
- items symbolizing what is special about the couple
- gifts

Choosing a Talking Piece:
- something symbolic of a union, love or the journey ahead (example: a special item of the couple's parents or grandparents)
- an item valued or chosen by the couple

Opening the Circle:
- light a candle and make a dedication.
- the couple lights a unity candle.
- the couple shares a story about how they met.
- the couple reads a selection written or chosen for the event.
- play special music chosen by the couple.

Questions for Circle Rounds:
- introduce yourself and share how you know the couple.
- share the story of any items brought for the center of the circle.
- tell a story about a quality such as humor that helps keep a relationship strong.
- what is a strength you see in each individual (of the couple) bringing to this relationship?

- relate a story about a lesson you have learned through a relationship.
- share a blessing you have received through a relationship.
- express your hopes for the couple.

Activities:
- see Celebration Wreath and Candle Wishes in the Activities section of the *Appendix.*
- Blessing of the Rings: at a friend's wedding, the bride and groom asked everyone attending, a small group of family and close friends, to stand in a circle. As the rings were passed around the circle, each person shared her/his hopes and blessings for the couple and the ceremony continued. At a large wedding, parents, grandparents and/or the wedding party could be asked to bless the rings as part of the ceremony.
- exchange of couple's vows

Closing the Circle:
- each person gives her/his best wishes for the couple.
- the couple share their closing thoughts.
- the couple moves to the center and everyone gives their blessings.
- present gifts.

Anniversary

An Anniversary Circle acknowledges and honors the journey a couple is sharing. Celebrating an anniversary typically highlights the number of years a couple has been together but it may also focus on the couple's accomplishments, hopes for the future or the history of their life together. An Anniversary Circle is an opportunity for family and friends to share what they appreciate about the couple and have learned from them. If your anniversary gathering includes too a large number of people for a circle, consider holding a smaller circle before or after the celebration.

Under each of the following headings, there are several suggestions listed. Choose which are appropriate for your gathering; consider those participating and the time you have available.

Creating a Center:
The host and/or participants may provide the following items. Place these items in the center before the circle and/or during a circle round.
- items symbolizing the couple's years together
- candles to honor the couple
- pictures of the wedding, past anniversaries or their life together
- special chocolates to be shared
- a beverage and glasses for a toast
- a wedding dress, jewelry and/or gifts reminiscent of the wedding day
- refer to suggestions under the Wedding/Union Circle

Choosing a Talking Piece:
- special item chosen by the couple
- a small gift presented at the beginning of circle
- an item representing a shared interest, a favorite trip or special memory
- a symbolic "tie that binds" (example: a ribbon tied or woven together)

Opening the Circle:
- read a selection chosen or written by the couple or each partner.
- the couple shares a story about how they met.
- family or friends read an inspirational poem written for the couple.
- play or sing a song that holds special meaning for the couple.
- see other suggestions under Wedding/Union Circle.

Questions for Circle Rounds:
- introduce yourself and share how you know the couple.
- share the story of any items brought for the center of the circle.
- share hopes for the couple's journey ahead.
- share something you value about the couple.
- see other suggestions under the Wedding/Union Circle.

Activities:

- see Celebration Wreath, Candle Wishes and Wall of Memories in the Activities section of the *Appendix*.

Closing the Circle:

- each partner or the couple presents a favorite reading.
- offer a toast with blessings for the couple.
- each person shares her/his wishes for the couple.

New Beginnings

New beginnings, planned or unplanned, often make us look at life differently. We may be leaving a relationship to begin life on our own, moving to a new location, starting a new job or simply setting new goals that will bring more dimension to life. With change there is often apprehension along with the excitement of discovering parts of ourselves we have not yet expressed.

Holding a circle to celebrate change highlights the possibilities before us. Sharing stories with others who have experienced what we are going through or simply being in the presence of those who care about us, helps us take our first steps in actualizing a new beginning.

This circle can be with a group sharing the same journey or for a person who wants to or has created a new beginning in her/his life. If including a meal or snacks, invite participants to create new recipes or bring familiar comfort foods.

Under each of the following headings, there are several suggestions listed. Choose which are appropriate for your gathering; consider those participating and the time you have available.

Creating a Center:

The host and/or participants may provide the following items. Place these items in the center before the circle and/or during a circle round.
- a nest with eggs to represent new life
- flowers, chocolates in a basket
- candles
- a new quilt or cloth to be presented to the honoree after circle
- items that represent new beginnings brought by each participant
- written stories about new beginnings in life
- a bowl where people place wishes for the honoree or new goals for themselves

Choosing a Talking Piece:
- a packet of seeds
- an egg, natural or made, from different materials such as stone or crystal
- a key to represent new doors that are opening
- an inspirational book about setting new goals or new beginnings

Opening the Circle:
- make a candle dedication for guidance, love and support for new beginnings.
- read a story or passage about new beginnings.
- the honoree shares what she/he envisions for herself/himself.

Questions for Circle Rounds:
- introduce yourself and share something that has recently come into your life that has brought you happiness.
- share the story of items brought and place them in the center.

- light your candle and honor a mentor who made a difference in your life.
- name a strength the honoree possesses (or one you have if the focus of circle includes the group).
- share an uncertainty you had before embarking on something new and how you worked through the challenges.
- share something you value or appreciate about the honoree.
- describe a funny moment you and the person being honored have shared.
- describe how humor has helped you through change.

Activities:
- empowerment exercise: each participant makes a statement about what she/he wants to create in life, writes it down, stating it in the positive and very specifically, then writes the affirmation as though it already exists – example: "I am successful at..." Take turns sharing in circle.
- see Appreciation, Art, Writing Activities and Sharing Values in the Activities section of the *Appendix*.
- each person does a reflection on the word "beginning" and shares its meaning in circle.

Closing the Circle:
- wishes and love are "sprinkled" on the honoree.
- everyone shares parting thoughts.
- pass the chocolates!
- refer to the list under Opening above.

People are hungry to be a part of something that is not a hierarchy because our culture today is full of it. Circle recognizes a more normal way of being. The shape is a big part of it – a big wheel with no beginning and no end. The format makes it different. It is a place to express tenderness. Now I see everything in circles - no wonder early cultures came up with circle - it brings us more in touch with nature. The connectedness of people in circle - about as connected as I can get with people outside my family.
— by Steve, circle participant

I was happy to be a part of the circle with friends. My concerns about attending were unfounded. I felt I had been a part of a deepened connection with people who I already knew well. It reminded me that there is always more to learn about and appreciate in others.

— by Linda, circle participant

I felt relaxed in circle, a sense of closeness to others, amazement at the insights shared, and a sense of freedom to say my mind in a safe environment.

— by Karen, circle participant

Imagination

Mystery

Change

Inspiration

Creativity

Discovery

Energy

Curiosity

Revelation

Vision

Understanding

The Green Sea Turtle Story

Sherry's Story

As a volunteer, I worked for a week with the Caribbean Conservation Corporation research team and their project with the endangered Green Sea Turtle in Costa Rica. Our work consisted of walking a remote beach during the night to take measurements and notes and tag females as they came to shore to lay eggs in the sand.

My grandson Bryce and I share a curiosity and enjoyment of nature so he reacted with excitement when I suggested I present my story to his first grade class. I wanted the children to be part of the presentation and create an experience they would remember – a circle would be the perfect way to share my story.

We placed a ceramic green turtle in a box with sawdust, simulating a real turtle in the sand. The sawdust needed to be deep, as the female digs a nest using her back flippers to lay about 100 white, glossy, Ping-Pong ball sized eggs. She then covers her nest with sand to protect them until it is time for them to hatch. We chose actual Ping-Pong balls for the eggs and a miniature turtle for the talking piece.

When I arrived at the classroom we gathered in circle on the floor around the turtle box. After the teacher introduced me and shared my purpose for coming, we rolled down the school map to locate where I had worked with the Green Sea Turtles and I shared pictures and my story about Green Sea Turtle research.

As we passed the talking piece, the students were asked to introduce themselves and tell a story about an animal they had helped. This was a way to introduce the importance of protecting animals and endangered species. It was interesting to observe how the talking piece helped the excited students take turns speaking.

Each student was handed a Ping-Pong ball and given a turn to place it in the nest to represent the eggs laid by the mother turtle. I read the story Follow the Moon, about a young boy who guards a turtle nest and guides freshly-hatched babies into the sea.

It captured the heart of my focus - the importance of taking care of nature so it continues to provide its great beauty and diversity.

The students were excited about what they learned. One of them observed my enthusiasm in the telling of my story, looked me in the eyes and exclaimed, "You really love turtles, don't you!" Some students were fascinated that turtles are green because they eat green sea grass and seaweed and they can rest underwater for several hours at a time!

The circle way of gathering offered a rich way to present this learning experience and an opportunity to enter and share the wonderment of first graders!

After the presentation, Bryce's commented that "The talking piece gave everyone a chance to talk when it came to them. I liked the information about how the body temperature determines if the turtle will be male or female when it is in the egg and learning that only one in one hundred turtles lives (makes it to maturity). It was weird – no interesting – how you brought the turtle in the box of sawdust. I would like to do another circle with a different topic, different animal, different species. Maybe we could go to the library and find another animal to do..."

Author's Note

The classroom was a great venue to hold a circle. Students were excited to share their experiences. The way they shared their stories, one person speaking at a time with the use of a talking piece, taught the value of listening more attentively. Each student had equal opportunity to talk but did not have to if she/he was uncomfortable doing so – but everyone was more than eager to share their stories about an animal they had helped in their lives.

The circle is a fun, interactive way to educate. In this circle, students learned about the green sea turtle through their careful listening, amazing curiosity, and questions.

What Are We Drawn To?
What Do We Want to Learn About?
What Nourishes Us?
Go For It!

These four discovery circles help us find the spark that energizes us to expand and strengthen our connections to the world around us. Our energy ebbs and flows throughout our lives. Sometimes we are aware of what sustains us and we seek it out. Other times we ignore or miss much of what is available to us. In these circles we expand our awareness about our hopes and dreams and explore ways to support and energize each other in the pursuit of these dreams. The following circles can be held individually, in some combination of each other, or planned as a series.

What Are We Drawn To? This circle helps us recognize and appreciate our relationship with the world around us. Before the circle, ask people to think about what they are drawn to now or at various times in their lives. This could be a person, place, idea, book, something in nature, a viewpoint – anything they notice and are drawn to. Discovering what we are drawn to highlights not only our sources of creativity and solace but also what holds meaning for us.

What Do We Want to Learn About? This is a circle to identify and explore something we want to know more about. Think about what intrigues you - what questions you keep asking. Sharing these questions with others keeps us in touch with our interests, our passions and what energizes us. It is a reminder that we all learn from each other. The group can discuss planning a second circle as a way to continue support and share learning.

What Nourishes Us? There are many sources for our energy - play, work, values, people, places, nature, learning, ideas, unexpected kindness, and spiritual life. This circle is an opportunity to highlight the importance of these forces in our lives. It helps us pay attention not only to what we are seeking but what we already have. Plan the circle to focus on a single topic such as a shared interest in gardening, photography, sports or nature, or open the circle to any topic by inviting each person to share what nourishes and replenishes her/his energy. Consider having a potluck dinner before or after the circle. Invite people to bring a favorite comfort food or to nourish their creativity by bringing something unusual.

Go For It! We all fantasize about possibilities but often keep them to ourselves. Those around us are not aware of our hopes and dreams. In this circle, each person reveals a dream or goal that is important to her/him. Sharing these dreams with others keeps them visible and encourages us to bring them into reality. Discuss holding additional circles to share ideas for moving forward and ways to support each other.

The above circles are similar in that they focus on revealing and sharing our interests and passions and finding ways to capture and direct the energy needed to live our lives fully. Because of these similarities, the suggestions given below can be used in more than one of the above circles. Choose those most appropriate for your focus or use your creativity and brainstorm other ideas.

Creating a Center:

The host and/or participants may provide the following items. Place these items in the center before the circle and/or during a circle round.

- items that represent the focus of the circles you are holding (example: an object or photograph of something you are drawn to, something you want to learn about or a source of energy).
- a symbol representing a goal each person wants to set for themselves
- pictures of inspiring people or activities

Choosing a Talking Piece:

- an item symbolic of something you are drawn to
- something that represents change, energy, adventure, possibility, knowledge, excitement, challenge, action or joy
- an item representing an inspirational place, person or something in nature
- something symbolic of the theme of discovery

Opening the Circle:

- share an inspirational reading, music, photograph or art work.
- read excerpts from an interview with a mentor or someone you admire.
- share an original writing or impromptu words from a circle participant.

Questions for Circle Rounds:

- introduce yourself and share something you love to do.
- share the story of any item you brought for the center.
- what are you drawn to? How is this a part of your life?
- what would you like to learn more about? How would you go about doing this?
- who or what supports your learning?
- what inspires you?
- who or what energizes you?
- what nourishes and guides your life?
- share a dream or goal.
- name two things you would like to better understand.
- have you ever come up with an idea for an invention? Share this experience.
- what gives you confidence?
- what is your greatest gift?
- share a personal strength that supports exploration or discovery in your life.

- who is or could be a mentor for you?
- when do you feel most alive?
- what are you doing when you lose all track of time?
- share a time when you overcame a challenge and achieved a goal.
- describe an experience that resulted in a shift in how you experienced or saw the world.

Activities:
- see Appreciation, Writing and Sharing Values under Activities in the *Appendix.*

Closing the Circle:
- each person shares an insight gained from circle and parting thoughts.
- circle members exchange views on holding a follow-up circle.
- see suggestions under Opening.

Thinking Outside the Box

Often in our lives we get stuck seeing things in the same way. While we need guideposts and familiarity, challenging ourselves to think outside the box opens us to new possibilities. It allows us to shift our perspectives giving us new and useful ways of seeing ourselves and the world around us.

At times we need to remind ourselves of the fun and energy we feel when we are creative. We benefit from activities that stimulate our creativity and give us permission to "think outside the box." This circle is designed to create such a space. It gives us an opportunity to challenge ourselves to think in new and different ways and to explore aspects of ourselves that we may not express.

Brainstorm with others how to make the circle as creative as possible. For example, you might ask everyone to dress in a new way - when we vary from our typical dress, it changes the way we and others see ourselves. Use your imagination to decorate and create the space in an unconventional way. Ask each person to bring a food item and then create a meal together without using a recipe. Or ask everyone to create a new recipe for a potluck or snack.

Under each of the following headings, there are several suggestions listed. Choose which are appropriate for your gathering; consider those participating and the time you have available.

Creating a Center:

The host and/or participants may provide the following items. Place these items in the center before the circle and/or during a circle round.
- items that represent creativity (examples: paints, camera, small building tools)
- items that can be put together in a variety of ways to create something new
- items that can have various uses
- miniature boxes with little tokens/gifts/words of inspiration for each participant
- a candle in a square container with a lid, symbolizing a box

Choosing a Talking Piece:
- an item symbolic of creativity (examples: paintbrush, a small building tool)
- a small, decorative, open box
- a miniature book with creative, inspirational passages
- an item chosen from those brought for the center

Opening the Circle:
- read an inspirational story about someone who thought outside the box.
- ask someone to write an opening about creativity.
- make a candle dedication to honor living out of our comfort zone.
- play or perform part of a favorite musical selection.
- perform a short drama.
- see Imagination Village described under Activities.

Questions for Circle Rounds:

- introduce yourself and share one word that describes your creativity.
- share any items brought for the center.
- share how your clothing represents the creative you (if participants were asked to dress in a way that represents their creativity).
- what stimulates and sustains your creativity?
- describe a time when you have thought outside the box.
- what is the most daring thing you have done?
- what is the most daring thing you would like to do?
- share a time when you experienced a shift in how you saw the world.
- what is something you have always wanted to do creatively?

Activities:

- create a place called Imagination Village by having each person describe what a town that supports creativity would look like (architecture, layout, activities, landscaping, government, businesses, schools, churches, parks). This could be a mental picture, a collage or a drawing on a large piece of paper. As part of the closing, participants could change or add to the picture. Share in circle.
- see *The Artist's Way* by Julia Cameron for additional activities.
- make available a variety of items to create sculptures, collages, paintings or digital photographs representing who you are or what you are doing when you are thinking outside the box.
- pass a familiar item around the circle - each person shares how it could be used in a different way.
- see Writing and Art in the Activities section in the *Appendix*.

Closing the Circle:

- share final thoughts and /or observations gained from circle.
- share any items made from a creative activity.
- present gifts contained in a box (see Creating Center).
- see suggestions under Opening above.

Show and Tell

Remember when we were little and we got to take our favorite things to school for show and tell? Sharing those items that held meaning in our lives brought a confirmation of who we were. Some of us even forgot our fear of standing up in front of everyone as we expressed our joy about what we brought. A Show and Tell Circle brings back that time in our lives when we had the floor and everyone really listened as we shared our stories.

The purpose of this circle is to help us recall the pure joy of showing and telling about people, experiences, and what is important in our lives. Planning a Show and Tell Circle with family, friends, and a cross section of ages is a fun way to learn more about each other. This circle could be repeated each year to show how we change.

Under each of the following headings, there are several suggestions listed. Choose which are appropriate for your gathering; consider those participating and the time you have available.

Creating a Center:

The host and/or participants may provide the following items. Place these items in the center before the circle and/or during a circle round.

- show and tell items
- childhood art work or art supplies
- tissue paper flowers in a vase
- a candle/s in bright colors or amusing shapes
- marbles placed inside a circle of string

Choosing a Talking Piece:

- a play microphone
- a box of crayons
- a paper hat or crown to place on the head of the person speaking
- a variation for the talking piece: the speaker may choose any item from the center she/he feels connected to. It can remain as a talking piece until someone wants to choose something different.

Opening the Circle:

- read a selection from the book *Everything I really need to know I Learned in Kindergarten* by Robert Fulghum.
- share a reading that acknowledges the child within.
- make a candle dedication to honor those who have truly listened to us in our life.

Questions for Circle Rounds:

- introduce yourself and share a funny childhood memory.
- share the story of any items brought for the center of the circle.

- recall a time you shared something important and someone truly listened.
- how do you "show and tell" about what is important to you today?
- relate a childhood experience of show and tell.
- recall a favorite childhood infatuation.
- share a funny childhood memory.
- what would you like others to know about your childhood years?
- what do you want to be when you grow up?

Activities:
- see Art and Word Reflection (do a word reflection on the phrase "show and tell") under Activities in the *Appendix*.

Closing the Circle:
- participants share their closing thoughts.
- read a passage on the value of listening to each other.
- honor those who have listened to our stories, today and in the past.
- each person extinguishes her/his candle and blesses the child within.

Play

Play is how children learn about themselves and their world. As adults, some of us forget the value and joy of losing ourselves in doing something we love. Being in this circle helps us rediscover and share how play and laughter contribute to our lives.

Create an atmosphere where everyone can relax and explore the fun and crazy in our imagined or real life. Invite people to wear something out of the ordinary or dress according to a particular theme. If a meal is planned, have people "play" at making new and unusual foods together. Think about a fun activity the group can do together. This could be an outdoor game or a creative activity – see Activities below.

Under each of the following headings, there are several suggestions listed. Choose which are appropriate for your gathering; consider those participating and the time you have available.

Creating a Center:

The host and/or participants may provide the following items. Place these items in the center before the circle and/or during a circle round.

- an item brought by each person that holds a special, fun memory
- items representing how you play or want to play
- something that makes you smile or laugh
- photographs of people in your life playing and laughing
- a photo of someone you know who has a great sense of humor

Choosing a Talking Piece

- a jack-in-the-box
- a small joke or magic book
- a funny image/picture
- a clown nose for the person whose turn it is to speak
- a variation for the talking piece: each person chooses an item from the center she/he feels connected to. It can remain as a talking piece until someone chooses something different.

Opening the Circle:

- share the quote, "Blessed are we who can laugh at ourselves for we shall never cease to be amused." Anonymous from *A Grateful Heart,* Ed. M.J. Ryan.
- read a selection about play or humor.
- sing a song with Kazoos or have instruments for each person; together play a favorite song such as Row, Row, Row Your Boat.
- read a humorous poem or reading.
- do a magic trick.
- tell a favorite joke.
- create and perform a skit.

Questions for Circle Rounds:
- introduce yourself and share the funniest thing that has happened to you recently.
- share the story about any items brought for the center of the circle.
- share a favorite fun or humorous memory.
- who or what makes you laugh?
- share what humor and/or play brings to your life.
- what is your favorite way to play?
- what brings out your playful, fun side?
- share something fun or crazy you have done or always wanted to do.
- share the significance of any special clothing worn.

Activities:
- make your funniest face - pass a mirror as you go around the circle so people can practice behind it before showing their final funny face.
- write funny action scenes on paper and put in a container; half of the group draws a scenario and, without talking, acts out their selection while the rest of group guesses the scene.
- do a charade of an animal family.
- have a squirt gun or water balloon fight.
- play a childhood game: hide and seek, ante over or pin the tail on the donkey – other suggestions are break a candy pinata or hold a puppet show.
- do a word reflection on the word "play."

Closing the Circle:
- each person creates a sentence that describes the circle. Someone writes these down and reads them back as a poem.
- each person reflects on how it felt to explore/express their playful side.
- see ideas under Opening.

Diva Delight

A Diva Delight is a circle to celebrate the feminine in a very expressive way. When we think of a "Diva" we often imagine it is someone who has reached acclaim for her talent and appears to revel in her role. This is what a Diva Delight Circle is about - over accentuating who we are or who we would like to be. It is an opportunity to explore our wild side and show up looking like it!

When we vary from our typical dress, it changes the way we see ourselves and how others see us. In this circle we can explore this in a safe and playful way.

Invite those who enjoy getting creative and want to bring out their extravagant side. This includes dressing accordingly, with lavish accouterments such as glittering jewels, bright dresses and elaborate hats. Participants can come dressed up or the hosts can provide a variety of items for participants to choose from after arriving. Ask participants to bring, or provide for them, props that add to the feeling of the exclusive diva such as boas and fake fur coats.

Under each of the following headings, there are several suggestions listed. Choose which are appropriate for your gathering; consider those participating and the time you have available.

Creating a Center:

The following items may be provided by the host and/or participants. These items may be placed in the center before the circle and/or during a circle round.

- bright colored cloth
- vibrant, artificial flowers
- candle/s
- boxes of chocolates
- unique cologne bottles
- antique gloves, purses and hats
- photos of "glamour girls"
- childhood or adult photos/stories of "hamming it up"

Choosing a Talking Piece:

- a ceramic, high heeled shoe
- a sequined heart
- a small book that plays on the theme of "Diva"

Opening:

- light a candle and make a dedication to everyone's feminine or wild side.
- share a reading from a book such as *I Am A Diva; Every Woman's Guide to Outrageous Living* by Elena Bates, Maureen O'Crean, Molly Thompson and Carilyn Vaile
- play music and do a "diva dance."

Questions for Circle Rounds:
- introduce yourself and describe the wildest thing you have ever worn and how it made you feel.
- share the story of any item you bought for the circle.
- what are you wearing when you feel your most outgoing?
- share a childhood memory of a glamorous role model.
- if you could dress like any woman in the world, who would it be?
- share a moment in life when you felt great about how you presented yourself.
- what is the most daring thing you have done?
- what is the most daring thing you would like to do?
- what characteristics about a female you admire would you like to incorporate into your life?

Activities:
- have a variety of hats, dresses, costumes and accessories available for people to try on when they arrive.
- ask each participants to write and describe what she would be doing if she could step out of her comfort zone or act outrageously. Share in circle.
- see Appreciation, A Gift for All, Art and Writing in the Activities section in the *Appendix*.

Closing:
- share your thoughts about the circle and any insight you have gained.
- see suggestions under Opening.

Time Travel

Is there a time period you would love to visit or even live in? Do you wonder how the world will change over the next one hundred, thousand or more years? Gather with others to explore your fantasies and curiosity about the past and the future. This is a circle for friends, families, and different ages. A school classroom might plan this circle as a group project to explore different time periods.

A Time Travel Circle is an opportunity for learning and creativity. Actively involve people of all ages by inviting them to collect information and/or create murals, skits or dioramas of different time periods.

Under each of the following headings, there are several suggestions listed. Choose which are appropriate for your gathering; consider those participating and the time you have available.

Creating a Center:
The host and/or participants may provide the following items. Place these items in the center before the circle and/or during a circle round.
- historical or futuristic items representing a time period (examples: toys, tools, pictures, books, events, music or art)
- items symbolic of time or the passage of time

Choosing a Talking Piece:
- choose an item from ideas listed under Creating a Center
- a watch

Opening the Circle:
- share a reading specific to a time period about a person, place or event.
- read a selection about the passage of time or time travel.
- share a fantasy about the future.
- share music or art from a specific time period.

Questions for Circle Rounds:
- introduce yourself as a person from a specific time period.
- share the story of any items brought for the center of the circle.
- what time period in the past or the future would you most like to live in or visit? What draws you to this time period? What draws you to that time period?
- how do you think the world will look in one hundred, five hundred or a thousand years from now? Describe one or more of the following for that specific time period: work, clothing, food, entertainment, travel, the environment, government, art, music, architecture.
- under which conditions do you forget time and place?
- when would you most like time to slow down or to speed up?

Activities:
- provide art materials, musical instruments and/or clothing for participants to create murals, posters, skits or dioramas about a historical or future time period. This can be done individually or in groups and then presented to the circle.
- see Writing and Art under Activities in the *Appendix*.
- have resources available such as historical time lines or predictions by futurists; take a break and invite participants to look up information about specific time periods - past or future. Return to circle and share with the group. Individuals or small groups might decide to collect this information before the circle. Encourage them to follow their own passions and interests. Their circle stories may inspire others to find out more about a time period and lead to a second circle to share more stories and information.

Closing the Circle:
- each person shares insights gained from the circle.
- see suggestions under Opening.

New Direction

Hope   Awareness

Potential   Fear

Discovery   **Transitions**   Renew

Trust   Change

Uncertainty   Awakening

Excitement

A House Blessing Story

Deborah's Story

I recently bought a new house and, for some reason, this one feels like home. I have owned a number of houses before and each one has had a name: the farmhouse, the duplex, the house in Princeton - but this one is called "home." Even though I'm alone and at times work to ward off loneliness, I want to fulfill a childhood dream of having a place of my own where I don't have to compromise my choices or accommodate space for things which are not mine. I don't know how long I want to be alone but it's time to fulfill this desire.

This house represents a new era in my life - one in which I am learning to take care of myself - emotionally, physically, mentally and spiritually. It may be in that spiritual sense that I thought I'd like to host a house blessing circle. Sherry gave me the framework of the circle and a few suggestions. I invited a small group of family and friends of about eight people to share the experience.

Starting with an explanation about the circle process, we followed with taking turns holding the talking piece as we introduced ourselves and shared our special memories of home. A candle, placed on a quilt my mother had made and given to me as a gift, formed the center of the circle. That, along with soft background music, gave the room a heartwarming energy where each person felt safe in "talking from the heart." Each shared memory added to the full dimension of the circle.

The small group size allowed everyone to feel comfortable sharing some of their intimate memories of home. Phil talked about living in the home where she was born and the choice she and her husband had made to stay there rather than move to a new house. Marcy talked about an endearing memory of her grandfather drawing a picture of a mouse on a chimney brick in the basement. My mom shared memories of how, as a child, she would sit in the stairwell to feel the glow of the sunshine on the red walls. After everyone shared their stories, we went into each room of the house, lit a candle and sounded a chime to bless the room.

My intention is to explore using spices more when cooking and baking in my new kitchen. To share some of the aromas that will soon fill my home, I passed a basket of various spices and each person selected two as a remembrance of the occasion.

My oldest daughter read a beautiful short book entitled "A House Blessing," a gift brought for me. We concluded the circle with my mom's story of the quilt she had made and given to me. Using the quilt in the circle was my way of honoring her.

It was a memorable ceremony for everyone who attended. Most had not heard of a house blessing before and were perhaps a bit apprehensive about the event but, after it was over, a couple of friends expressed an interest in hosting a house blessing for someone special to them. It was a ceremony we will all hold dear to our hearts

Author's Note

A circle gathering adds a new dimension to house blessings - an opportunity for those attending to share their thoughts of home and what that means to them. This circle was a highly interactive gathering where distant memories were recalled and shared with the group.

In the process of planning the circle, Deborah articulated her thoughts about where she was in her life and what she wanted for her future. Circle became a way for her to express that by sharing something that represented life in her new home – her desire to explore the use of spices in cooking.

Deborah's family shared in the presentation of circle, making it a cross-generational experience that gave participants an opportunity to know more about Deborah and her family's shared history. The reading of the book by her daughter and the circle closing were a spontaneous decision made during circle, demonstrating that not everything needs to be planned thoroughly before coming together.

Graduation

Graduation is a time of reflection and looking ahead to new goals. A circle creates the perfect space to do both. Verbalizing our hopes and plans in the presence of others helps us clarify and confirm what is important in our lives. As we listen to each person in circle, we sift through our thoughts and filter out what is relevant to us. Our stories offer inspiration to the new graduate as she/he moves into a new chapter of life.

Invite the graduate to help plan the Graduation Circle. This circle can focus on the journey ahead, specific accomplishments, or it can simply be a time to share stories about the graduate. The circle also gives the graduate an opportunity to thank those present for their support throughout the school years and to share her/his thoughts on graduating or goals for the future.

The circle could be held with a small group of family and friends right before a traditional, larger gathering or as the graduation celebration itself. Including elders and young children adds a wonderful dimension to the celebration.

Under each of the following headings, there are several suggestions listed. Choose which are appropriate for your gathering; consider those participating and the time you have available.

Creating a Center:
The host and/or participants may provide the following items. Place these items in the center before the circle and/or during a circle round.
- pictures of the graduate at different ages
- candles, items from nature, flowers
- items representing significant moments, events or accomplishments
- written memories or wishes for the graduate
- gifts for the graduate
- gifts or words presented by the graduate to each person thanking her/him for support

Choosing a Talking Piece:
- something of value chosen by the graduate
- an item representing an accomplishment or special interest of the graduate
- an item symbolic of a wish for the graduate
- a small gift, wrapped or unwrapped
- something created by or for the guest of honor

Opening the Circle:
- relate a story about the accomplishments of the graduate.
- light a candle and make a dedication to honor the graduate.
- share a reading or special music chosen by the graduate.

Questions for Circle Rounds:

- introduce yourself and share a story of how you know the graduate.
- share the story of any items brought for the circle.
- relate a special memory about the graduate.
- name a personal strength of the honoree that you value.
- share something you looked forward to after your graduation.
- what is a lesson you learned from a teacher/mentor/friend?
- what inspires you and helps you reach your goals?
- describe something that brought you out of your comfort zone.
- share a time when there was a shift in how you saw the world.

Activities:

- see Appreciation, Celebration Wreath, Candle Wishes and Wall of Memories under Activities in the *Appendix*.

Closing the Circle:

- each person expresses her/his well wishes or blessings for the graduate.
- the graduate reads a favorite passage.
- the graduate shares her/his goals or hopes for the future.
- give a round of applause for the graduate.
- present gifts.

Rite of Passage

There are special times in our lives that define a passage from one stage of life to another. The acknowledgment of these passages may be rooted in cultural, spiritual, or religious traditions. The right to drive, a first hunting experience, the onset of menses, starting our first job, or turning the legal adult age are important moments in our lives. An adult brings additional rites of passages such as becoming independent of parents, significant birthdays, marriage, divorce, job changes or promotions and menopause for women. By sharing our stories about how we move through these transitions, we celebrate and acknowledge both the rewards and challenges that come with change.

This circle honors a rite of passage but also provides support if needed. It may focus on the next stage of life and how perspectives can change with the passing of time. The circle also provides an opportunity to find closure by letting go of those parts of our lives we are ready to leave behind.

Plan this circle to honor either an individual's rite of passage or a group of people who want to reflect on a shared passage in life. If one person is being honored, consider inviting people of different ages. The setting could be a home, a public or spiritual facility, a place in nature, or anywhere that is appropriate for those involved.

Under each of the following headings, there are several suggestions listed. Choose which are appropriate for your gathering; consider those participating and the time you have available.

Creating a Center:

The host and/or participants may provide the following items. Place these items in the center before the circle and/or during a circle round.
- a handmade quilt
- items or photos reflecting the person/s journey in life
- items symbolic of the transition being honored
- candle/s
- the model of a bridge
- favorite childhood/young adult items
- gifts/tokens

Choosing a Talking Piece:
- a symbol of the rite of passage (example: a symbol of faith for spiritual passages, keys to the car or drivers license when starting to drive, a picture or small book that reflects the new stage of life)
- something of value brought by the person being honored
- an item created by an individual or collectively by participants
- a small book of well wishes for the person being honored

Opening the Circle:
- share a story about a rite of passage.
- light a candle with a dedication to the rite of passage.
- read a favorite selection chosen by the person/s being honored.

Questions for Circle Rounds:
- introduce yourself and share a funny story about a rite of passage or transition.
- tell the story of the item brought and place it in the center.
- light a candle and share your wishes for the person being honored or for yourself as you make this rite of passage in life.
- share a story about your apprehensions before or as you moved through this rite of passage. Looking back, were they realistic? Did your apprehensions serve you in some way?
- what are some things others told you about this rite of passage? Are they true for you?
- share a blessing you received from this rite of passage in your life.
- name one characteristic you most like about the person being honored/yourself.
- what are some of your strengths that have served you in making this rite of passage?
- what new responsibilities came with this rite of passage?
- do you view yourself differently now? Do others?
- what are some of the things you have learned about yourself?
- recall a challenge you overcame to arrive at this point in life.
- what is one thing you would like to pass on to others that would help them make this rite of passage?

Activities:
- see Appreciation, Art, Writing and Sharing Values listed under Activities in the *Appendix*.

Closing the Circle:
- each person shares parting thoughts.
- share a reading or give a blessing that honors what was learned in this rite of passage.
- participants blow out their candles and share a wish for the future.
- present gifts.

Moving

Leaving one's home, neighborhood, or place of work to relocate can be a life-changing experience. While it may represent a fresh start, it could also be difficult to leave friends, family or coworkers. Holding a circle offers a way for all to come together to express their support and share well wishes and parting thoughts.

The circle can focus on ways to keep in contact, what one has valued about the relationship/s, how the relocation came about, the positive changes coming with the move, and offers of physical support to help with the move. The person or persons being honored can be asked which focus would be most meaningful and how much they would like to participate in planning the circle. The circle is also an opportunity for them to express appreciation for the friendship and support they have received. A potluck with the honoree's favorite foods helps create more time for visiting.

Under each of the following headings, there are several suggestions listed. Choose which are appropriate for your gathering; consider those participating and the time you have available.

Creating a Center:
The host and/or participants may provide the following items. Place these items in the center before the circle and/or during a circle round.
- a candle/s
- pictures of the new home or place of work
- favorite photographs
- items representing the relationship or a shared experience with the person/s being honored
- road map with the journey to the new location marked
- gifts (examples: self-addressed stamped card with envelopes, calling cards with telephone number attached)

Choosing a Talking Piece:
- something of value chosen by the person/s moving
- a symbol of friendship or love
- a small book that includes well wishes written by each person present
- an item representing the move (examples; a toy truck, a suitcase charm)

Opening the Circle:
- light a candle for "illuminating the path for the new journey."
- share a favorite reading chosen by the person/s moving.
- read a short selection about the positive aspects of change.
- the person moving shares a story about her/his relocation.

Questions for Circle Rounds:
- introduce yourself and share how you know the guest/s of honor.

- share the story of any items brought for the center of the circle.
- express what you value about the person/s being honored.
- relate something you have learned from the person/s moving.
- recall a funny story about the person/s being honored.
- share a experience from one of your past moves.
- the honoree/s express their thoughts or appreciation to each person holding the talking piece.

Activities:
- see Appreciation, A Gift Sharing, Wall of Memories and Art (make a collage of memories) under Activities in the *Appendix*.

Closing the Circle:
- read a collection of well wishes from the group.
- the honoree chooses and reads a passage or shares her/his thoughts.
- guest/s of honor step inside the circle and everyone uses hand gestures to "sprinkle" them with love and blessings.
- present gifts.

House Warming/Blessing

This circle creates a gathering that, in a phrase from the past, "warms the house." It can celebrate the transition to a new residence or the beginning of life in a person's first home. A wide range of people including family, friends, and old and new neighbors could be invited.

Plan the circle with the homeowner/s; discuss whom to invite, who will bring the talking piece and if there is something about their new home they want to highlight. Decide if everyone will bring a snack or if the honoree/s would enjoy preparing something. This is also an opportunity to acknowledge appreciation for those who have provided support. Refer to "A House Blessing Story" earlier in this section that describes using a circle for a House Blessing.

Under each of the following headings, there are several suggestions listed. Choose which are appropriate for your gathering; consider those participating and the time you have available.

Creating a Center:

The host and/or participants may provide the following items. Place these items in the center before the circle and/or during a circle round.

- a small, handmade quilt or wall hanging
- items representing the meaning of home
- a candle/s, fresh flowers or other items from nature
- a small book containing well wishes from each participant
- favorite photographs
- gifts for the home
- a collection of addresses and phone numbers from participants of the circle
- copies of a favorite poem or reading chosen by the guest/s of honor

Choosing a Talking Piece:

- a valued item selected by person/s being honored
- something that represents the significance of the move or the new home

Opening the Circle:

- share the story of how the guest/s of honor came to live in their home.
- read a selection about the meaning of home.
- make a candle dedication to "bring light and warmth to the home."
- share a favorite poem, inspirational reading or music selected by the person/s being honored.

Questions for Circle Rounds:

- introduce yourself and share how you know the guest/s of honor.
- share the story of any item you brought for the center of the circle.
- share a story about a favorite home or a place that felt like home.
- what does the word "home" mean to you?

- share your hopes for the person/s in the new home.
- share your thoughts on what makes a home.

Activities:
- do a house tour and bless each room by lighting a candle to "bring warmth and light" to the space.
- ringing a bell or sounding a chime followed by a moment of silence.
- reading a poem or blessing.
- plan a word reflection on the meaning of the word "home." See Word Reflection under Activities in the *Appendix*.

Closing the Circle:
- each person or the host gives a blessings for the new home and those who live there.
- the person/s honored give a reading that holds special significance to them.
- share a message about the meaning of home (example: read *A House Blessing* by Welleran Poltarness - everyone sign it and present as a gift).

Empty Nest

Are you or another parent experiencing a mix of feelings that comes when the last child leaves home? Even as we look forward to more time and freedom for ourselves, we may be asking, "What now?"

An "empty nest" is an opportunity to revisit interests and activities that we put on hold while doing the important job of raising our children. It is a time to celebrate the skills and knowledge we have gained along with the gifts we have given and received from our children. In this circle, we support each other by sharing stories that acknowledge the possibilities that lie before us.

Gather a group of parents who are new empty nesters or invite a combination of parents, friends, children and family to the circle. If a meal is planned, invite people to use their creativity and bring something they have never prepared. If including an activity such as having each person create a picture or collage of possibilities, provide supplies, or ask others to bring the items they will need.

Under each of the following headings, there are several suggestions listed. Choose which are appropriate for your gathering; consider those involved and the time you have available.

Creating a Center:
The host and/or participants may provide the following items. Place these items in the center before the circle and/or during a circle round.
- a container or nest (if large enough, it can be used to hold items placed in the center)
- a candle/s
- items symbolic of what you look forward to as an empty nester
- items representing an interest or goal you want to pursue

Choosing a Talking Piece:
- an egg to represent new beginnings
- a symbol of a sun to represent new energy and light
- an item chosen from those placed in the center

Opening the Circle:
- share an inspirational reading.
- make a candle dedication to honor what has gone before and the journey ahead.
- read a humorous poem about change.
- share a reading about acceptance, change or transformation.

Questions for Circle Rounds:
- introduce yourself and share what you have most enjoyed about being a parent.
- share the story about any item you brought for the center.

- share a story about what you have learned from raising children and how this enriches your life as you move on.
- describe an interest or goal you want to pursue.
- what are some of the gifts you have given to your child/children?
- what are some of the gifts your child/children have given to you?
- describe a favorite place, activity or interest and share what you like about it.
- what brings you joy?
- are you a risk taker? When?
- share something you have always wanted to do.
- share how you will relate to those who have left the nest.

Activities:
- see Art, Word Reflection and Sharing Values in the Activity section of the *Appendix.*

Closing the Circle:
- share insights gained from the circle.
- see suggestions under Opening.

Retirement

Retirement is a time of transition. It may be a welcomed event and, at the same time, create uncertainties about the future as we move from one phase of life to another. It is a time to both celebrate and explore the opportunities that lie ahead. Circle gatherings provide support for the transition and offer a way to honor this stage in our lives.

This circle can focus on many aspects of retirement: honoring work accomplished, pursuit of new interests, or how the retiree feels about this transition. If there is hesitancy about retiring, the circle can offer support and help explore options. Ask the retiree what kind of circle would be meaningful, where it could be held, and whom to invite. Also ask her/him to choose something with special meaning to use as a talking piece. If time permits, include a meal or snack that features favorite dishes of the retiree.

Under each of the following headings, there are several suggestions listed. Choose which are appropriate for your gathering; consider those participating and the time you have available.

Creating a Center:

The host and/or participants may provide the following items. Place these items in the center before the circle and/or during a circle round.

- items that highlight the retiree's future (examples: sport equipment, favorite books, travel)
- a basket of well wishes from employees, friends or family
- invitations to get together with the retiree
- collection of addresses, e-mail and phone numbers of coworkers and friends
- flowers or a special candle for the retiree
- a gift certificate to a fitness center
- a box of chocolates, cake or gifts to share
- a beverage with special glasses

Choosing a Talking Piece:

- an item symbolizing the retiree's contribution in the work place
- a valued item chosen by the retiree
- an item reflecting a new or ongoing interest for the retiree (examples: sewing, fishing or travel)
- a small book that celebrates retirement
- the proverbial gold watch (a real or play one)
- a walking stick for her/his travels

Opening the Circle:

- share a reading selected by the retiree or another participant.
- make a candle dedication that honors the new opportunities for the retiree.

- the retiree shares a story about one of her/his best work experiences.
- if available, shred the retiree's old job application.

Questions for Circle Rounds:
- introduce yourself and describe when you met or how you know the retiree.
- share the story of any items brought for the center of the circle.
- name something you appreciate or value about the retiree.
- share a funny story about the retiree.
- name a strength she/he possesses.
- share how you are planning for retirement. If you have retired, share some challenges or successes.
- the honoree shares what she/he would like to do after retirement.

Activities:
- write well wishes on a banner/card as it is passed around the circle.
- see Celebration Wreath, Candle Wishes, Wall of Memories and Word Reflection (on the word retire) listed under Activities in the *Appendix*.

Closing the Circle:
- each person shares wishes for the retiree.
- the retiree selects or writes a passage and shares it.
- present any gifts.
- do a "hip-hip-hooray" toast for the retiree.

When somebody actually listens to us, it creates us, it makes us unfold and expand and ideas actually begin to grow within us and come to life. *A Thousand Paths to Tranquility* .

— by David Baird

I believe that we all have a memory of living in a circle there in our genes. For over a million years human beings everywhere lived in circle, close to each other and in harmony with nature. *The Circle Way.*

— by Manitonquat

I felt very good about who I am and part of a growing experience for all who were at circle. There was a real closeness and a renewal of friendships. I liked the use of the talking piece. It gave me an opportunity to really <u>hear</u> people's stories and thoughts.

— by Carole, circle participant

Possibilities

Excitement   Preparation

Map   Companionship

Step by Step   Life

The Journey

Comfort Zone   Detours

Growth   Insight

Baggage   Destination

Spirit

Life Celebration Story

This circle was held to honor a special friend Ginny, struggling with multiple sclerosis for years, and to celebrate the life of her sister Roberta, who had recently passed away from cancer. Ginny, Roberta and their sister Margaret made up "the three Moore sisters." Their antics have provided their friends with hilarious and engaging stories over the years; they have been a treasured three. The day we chose for holding the circle happened to be Margaret's birthday, so the circle became a wonderful opportunity to celebrate all three of the Moore sisters.

Margaret's Story

Never have I been so lonesome as I was on September 27, 2002, sitting in a hotel room in San Francisco by myself, writing a eulogy on hotel stationary for my sister Roberta's memorial service the next day. Saddened by her death, after a courageous battle from cancer, I felt peace knowing she was now free from all her pain and suffering. While that helped, I really needed a friend to comfort me.

The friend I needed was my younger sister, Ginny, who was laying in the CCU unit at a hospital a few miles away after suffering respiratory arrest shortly after arriving in San Francisco. She was to spend three months in the hospital, slowly recovering from pneumonia complicated by her condition of multiple sclerosis. Her husband Jim, always at her side, kept her family and friends updated on her progress.

In late June Ginny was able to fly to Minnesota to her beloved summer home on Ten Mile Lake close to the town of Walker where she was born and raised. We scattered Roberta's ashes in Ten Mile on one sunny day in July. Ginny was finally given some closure to Roberta's death with the special service she had planned.

At last, I had my special friend, my sister Ginny, getting healthy, going shopping and being able to visit with her friends from Walker and Princeton, Minnesota, where she and her husband Jim lived for many years and raised their two sons.

Their good friends from Princeton planned a circle for Ginny at her lake home on August 14th. They brought all the food and each guest was asked to bring a memory symbolizing their friendship with Ginny and Roberta. I brought pictures of my two sisters and a black dress that belonged to Roberta, which she had given me. The dress draped an empty chair in the circle to represent her presence.

My daughters asked me how the day went. The best words I could use to describe it were "tearful" and "joyful." A toy, a stuffed loon so reminiscent of Ten Mile Lake, was chosen as our talking piece. It was passed around and the guest holding the loon shared stories and memories of Roberta and Ginny. The women in that circle cared: they laughed and cried - emotions that expressed the true meaning of friendship and bonds that are broken but never lost from a friend's passing. In writing this, one thinks of one's own mortality and the reaction of friends.

I am no longer so lonely. I miss Roberta, but Ginny and I have formed a strong healing bond and that circle of friends that met in August will never be forgotten.

Linda's Story

What impressed me most about Ginny's circle was how it brought together two groups of people who had never met - half from Ginny's youth in Walker, MN, and half from her adult years in Princeton. As we each took our time with the talking piece, I felt such a connection with people I had never known, because I so understood their words about Ginny and her sisters Roberta and Margaret.

Something that is so amazing about circle - we learn/gain so much by honoring others. I wasn't sure if I actually could articulate anything, even though I am rarely at a loss for words! I was almost ready to pass but suddenly, when I received the talking piece, it didn't matter if I said it well; I simply needed to say it. After the circle, someone said she had no idea what was involved in circle and was amazed that people who had never met could share so openly. She also commented how nervous she was about having to talk and how glad she was to have had the chance. Several commented about how they 'dared' to say things they hadn't anticipated saying, given the non-threatening, encouraging atmosphere of circle.

It was a wonderful example of the meaning of circle: the essential human connection through our shared emotions of love, sorrow, joy, hope and fear. We were provided a comfortable environment in which to share all of the above in celebration of the Moore Sisters. How wonderful it would have been to have had all three Moore sisters physically there, but what an important opportunity to continue healing amidst the celebration.

Author's Note

One of the ways we honor people we love is to celebrate them. Creating a circle with this intention is one of the easiest, yet personal and memorable way to do this. Everyone was simply asked to bring something that reminded them of Ginny. In the center we placed a cloth with a cake made of flowers, a candle with three wicks (to acknowledge the three sisters), and pictures and personal items that Ginny chose.

The loon talking piece went around the circle only once as each participant shared their stories about their history with Ginny. Because the participants knew Ginny's at different times of her life, everyone got a glimpse of her past and present. Pictures were taken before circle as a meal was prepared, some taken during and after circle and were later presented to Ginny in an album.

Linda's additional remarks reflect on the gifts we receive as participants of circle; learning more about each other and feeling free to express ourselves in a safe environment.

Accomplishments

When we accomplish something special in our lives, sharing it with people we care about enriches our experience. A circle that celebrates an accomplishment offers others an opportunity to share congratulations and stories about the person or group being honored. It is also an ideal time to express thanks to those who provided support and encouragement.

There are many accomplishments in life to celebrate, such as a promotion at work, developing a healthier life style, healing a relationship, or reaching any important goal. When planning this circle, visit with those being honored for their ideas on who and what they would like to include in the celebration.

Under each of the following headings, there are several suggestions listed. Choose which are appropriate for your gathering; consider those participating and the time you have available.

Creating a Center:
The host and/or participants may provide the following items. Place these items in the center before the circle and/or during a circle round.
- photos or items marking the stages in accomplishing the goal
- candles, items from nature, flowers
- gifts for the person/s being honored
- written wishes for those being honored
- tokens/gifts

Choosing a Talking Piece:
- a medal, award or something symbolic of the accomplishment
- a small gift
- an item brought by the person/s being honored
- an item created for those being honored

Opening the Circle:
- light a candle and make a dedication to the honoree.
- tell a story/stories about the accomplishment.
- share a reading or music selection chosen by the one being honored.

Questions for Circle Rounds:
- introduce yourself and share how you know the guest/s of honor.
- share the story of any items brought for the center of the circle.
- share your wishes for the person/s being honored.
- what is one of your most significant accomplishments in life?
- how have others been positively affected by the accomplishment?
- what helped you reach an important goal?
- who do you want to thank for their support?
- share a time you overcame a challenge.

- who has been an influential mentor for you?
- how has someone inspired you to set and/or meet a goal?

Activities:
- see Celebration Wreath, Appreciation, and Candle Wishes in the Activities section of the *Appendix*.

Closing the Circle:
- each person expresses her/his wishes or blessings for the honoree.
- share words of congratulations.
- the honoree expresses thanks for the support received.
- the person being honored shares the new goals she/he is considering.
- present gifts.

Wisdom

How do we gain wisdom? Is it through people we know, books we read or simply by observing life? Is it through our experiences, through stories handed down from generation to generation, or through our interactions with the world around us? If we think about it, we learn through each of these. We consciously choose things we want to learn, but we also learn intuitively without realizing it. Whenever we are listening, reading, interacting, expressing or observing, we are learning. Everything and every person can be our teacher.

In a wisdom circle we learn from each other. As we hear others speak and are listened to, we learn new ways to look at life and deepen our understanding of each other. Sharing our knowledge and searching for understanding connects us to others and helps us take one more step on our journey in life.

Inviting participants from all ages and stages of life brings a rich balance to a wisdom circle. Children bring wonderful and fresh insights to any topic. Elders offer their wisdom based on years of experience. This circle can have a particular focus such as how we learn from each other, gain knowledge about a particular subject, or it can simply honor the wisdom and experience of those present or others important in our lives.

The circle might be the entire event or held as part of another gathering. At a reunion this circle could honor elders and the wisdom they bring to the family. It could be held within a school, organization or workplace to honor mentors or teachers for their guidance and for sharing their knowledge.

Under each of the following headings, there are several suggestions listed. Choose which are appropriate for your gathering; consider those participating and the time you have available.

Creating a Center:
The host and/or participants may provide the following items. Place these items in the center before the circle and/or during a circle round.
- items that represent sources of wisdom (example: books, photos of mentors or teachers, something from nature)
- candle/s
- a key to represent the unlocking of our minds
- photographs of inspirational people or places
- gifts

Choosing a Talking Piece:
- something symbolic of wisdom and learning
- an item to be given as a gift if a person/s are being honored.
- a valued item brought by an elder

Opening the Circle:
- share an inspirational reading or music.

- read a quote/s from a person admired for their wisdom.
- make a candle dedication to wisdom and the joy of learning.

Questions for Circle Rounds:
- introduce yourself and share something important you learned recently.
- light a candle and silently or verbally honor someone who has been a mentor to you.
- share the story of any items brought for the center.
- recall a time a mentor or teacher made a difference in your life.
- who has served as a role model for you?
- share sources of wisdom in your life.
- name a person you would like to learn more from.
- who do you think is one of the wisest people in history?
- share something you would like to learn about.
- what inspires you?
- what is one lesson you wish you could teach the next generation?
- what have you learned from the person being honored?
- what do you do to enhance or support your own learning?

Activities:
- see Sharing Values and Word Reflection in the Activities section of the *Appendix*.

Closing the Circle:
- each person shares her/his insights gained from the circle.
- participants blow out their candles and offer a blessing for their sources of wisdom.
- see suggestions above under Opening.

Gratitude

We are so busy in our day-to-day activities we seldom stop to notice the many things we are thankful for in our lives. Our focus is more often on what needs to be done and how we are going to navigate life each day. When we stop to recall and acknowledge our blessings, we become aware of the abundance in our lives and our spirits are lifted.

This circle provides an opportunity to slow down, refocus, and express our gratitude for our blessings. In doing so, we learn to appreciate who we are, our importance to each other, and where we are in the journey of life.

The focus for this circle could simply be "gratitude" or you may decide to choose a particular focus that is not ordinarily celebrated such as the gift of friendship, honoring the beauty of nature, or celebrating the support of family and friends. To create a more meaningful time together, the question "What are you grateful for?" could be used as a spontaneous circle round when a group is together for a meal.

Under each of the following headings, there are several suggestions listed. Choose which are appropriate for your gathering; consider those participating and the time you have available.

Creating a Center:
The host and/or participants may provide the following items. Place these items in the center before the circle and/or during a circle round.
- candle/s
- flowers or other items from nature
- item/s reflecting something you are grateful for
- copies of a special poem or passage
- gifts or tokens

Choosing a Talking Piece:
- an item representing something a person is grateful for
- a small book on gratitude that could be read as an opening or closing
- an item relating to a particular circle focus you may choose (examples: friendship or nature)

Opening the Circle:
- share a reading, writing or spontaneous words about gratitude or appreciation.
- light a candle and make a dedication to honor what we are grateful for in our lives.

Questions for Circle Rounds:
- introduce yourself and recall a recent blessing or something you have done that has brought you happiness.

- share the story of any items brought for the center of the circle.
- share how a teacher or mentor has been instrumental in your life (individual candles may be lit if brought, and placed in the center).
- what are you most grateful for?
- recall a favorite event or time in life.
- what do you most appreciate about yourself? Family? Friends?
- what is one gift you give to yourself? To others?
- name something you want to bring into your life to make it richer.
- share a story about something difficult that turned into a blessing.
- where is your favorite place in nature?
- what has been your favorite vacation. Why?

Activities:
- see Appreciation, A Gift Sharing, Word Reflection and Art (create a collage of blessings) described in the Activities section of the *Appendix*.

Closing the Circle:
- participants give closing comments and reflections on the circle.
- everyone shares one thing they appreciate about themselves.
- share a reading about finding gratitude in everyday life.
- present gifts.

A Retreat

We honor ourselves and enhance our relationships when we take time for personal growth. A Retreat Circle offers a safe and welcoming place to do this. When we create a space that welcomes our authentic self, we honor our spirit. Consider where you have felt the most secure in expressing your thoughts and have gained personal insight. Isn't it in a place free from criticism that allows full expression and time to reflect? A Retreat Circle creates such a space.

This circle can be a two to three hour gathering or a full day or weekend retreat that includes a variety of activities and/or body therapy. Refer to "Summer Solstice Celebration" under *Circle Stories* earlier in the book for a story about this kind of circle. For additional ideas refer to the circle Who Am I, Who Am I Becoming and the first four circles under the Discovery theme.

Under each of the following headings, there are several suggestions listed. Choose which are appropriate for your gathering; consider those participating and the time you have available.

Creating a Center:
The host and/or participants may provide the following items. Place these items in the center before the circle and/or during a circle round.
- a cloth for the floor or a low table
- something from nature (examples: flowers, stones, pine cones)
- candle/s
- an item/s reflecting personal growth (examples: pictures, symbols, creative art/writing)
- a small item that represents happiness in your life
- handouts: information on health/nutrition, copies of poems, quotes or favorite writings

Choosing a Talking Piece:
- an item from nature
- a crystal, stone or ceramic heart
- symbols of healing, friendship, love, well being or personal growth

Opening the Circle:
- ring a chime or bell to signify the beginning of circle.
- share music, dance or drumming.
- do a short guided meditation (refer to Activities below).
- have a moment of silence.
- do breath work or stretching exercises.
- read a passage reflecting the focus of the circle such as renewal, well being or personal growth.
- light a candle and make a dedication for renewal, well being, finding beauty within or trusting intuition

- everyone stand and turn to the right, facing the same direction. Snug up the circle and place hands on the shoulders of the person in front. Rub their back. Turn to the other direction and rub the back of the person in front. Make sure participants of your circle will be comfortable with touching before you engage in this activity.

Questions for Circle Rounds:
- introduce yourself and share a recent blessing.
- share the story of the item you brought for the center.
- light your candle to honor a mentor/teacher and share how they influenced your life.
- what makes you laugh?
- what inspires you?
- what is your passion?
- what are you curious about or want to learn more about?
- what thrills you?
- what gives you confidence?
- what are you most grateful for?
- what is your greatest gift to yourself? To others?
- what do you do to nurture yourself? What would you like to do?
- what do you fear the most?
- what helps you be couragous?
- in what situations do you present a false self to others?
- what do you most appreciate about your self?
- what has been your greatest adventure?
- what is one thing you would like to improve about your life?
- what one person has been the most influential in your life?
- what do you want to be doing five years from now?
- what would you like written on your tombstone?
- see "Books With Questions for Circle Rounds" in the *Circle Resources* section.

Activities:
- a guided meditation. Author Shakti Gawain offers examples to use in many of her books including *Creative Visualization*. Follow with participants sharing their insights in circle.
- a reflective writing. Journal on any of the Questions for Circle Rounds listed above.
- empowerment exercise: each participant makes a statement about what she/he wants to create in life, writes it down, stating it in the positive and very specifically, then writes the affirmation as though it already exists – example: "I am successful at ..." Take turns sharing in circle.
- all activities in the Activities section of the *Appendix* can be adapted.

- for additional ideas check Jennifer Louden's book *The Woman's Retreat Book; a Guide to Restoring, Rediscovering, and Reawakening Your True Self – in a Moment, an Hour, a Day, or a Weekend* or Robin Deen and Sally Craig's book, *Sacred Circles: A Guide to Creating Your Own Women's Spirituality*.

Closing the Circle:
- read an inspirational passage or poem together.
- each person gives her/his reflections or insights from the gathering.
- create a song to a common tune and sing together.
- stand together connected, in silence.

Healthy Living

Our lives are filled with choices. This circle is about celebrating those choices that have a positive impact on our health and well being. How we think about this varies. Some of us focus mainly on diet and exercise. Others include how work, play, and spiritual life contribute to health. In this circle, we share our views on what healthy living means to us along with our ideas and experiences about nutritious food, exercise and other activities that support well-being.

Plan an activity that involves physical exercise or stress reducing activities such as relaxation techniques, meditation, or yoga. The group can exchange tasty and healthy recipes and enjoy a potluck including these dishes. Another idea is to have each person bring one healthy ingredient to create a soup, stew, or other dish together.

This could be a one-time circle, part of another circle such as Family Night, or an ongoing gathering of people who want to emphasize healthy choices in their lives. It could also be part of a day retreat where spa treatments are included along with other activities. See A Retreat Circle for more ideas.

Under each of the following headings, there are several suggestions listed. Choose which are appropriate for your gathering; consider the number participating and the time you have available.

Creating a Center:
The host and/or participants may provide the following items. Place these items in the center before the circle and/or during a circle round.
- items that represent health (physical, mental, or spiritual)
- nutritional bars/snacks
- resource book or list of local health/exercise services
- favorite health, exercise or mind-body-spirit books to share with everyone
- handouts: information on health/nutrition

Choosing a Talking Piece:
- a stone, crystal or ceramic heart
- a symbol of the human form
- an item representing healthy living
- a medal/award from an accomplishment
- an item chosen from those placed in the center

Opening the Circle:
- play a short selection of relaxing music.
- introduce a deep breathing or stretching exercise.
- read an inspirational story about attaining a healthy lifestyle.
- share a reading that reflects the value or enjoyment of caring for oneself.
- encourage everyone to let go of negative images of self followed by a moment of silence.

Questions for Circle Rounds:
- introduce yourself and share something you have done recently that brought you happiness.
- share stories of items brought for the center.
- share what you presently do that contributes to your well being.
- what are some healthy goals you would like to set for yourself?
- what helps you make healthy choices?
- what do you love doing? How is this part of your feeling healthy?
- how can those present support your healthy choices?
- what do you need to learn about to improve your well being? How can you do this?
- name the most enjoyable physical thing you have done.
- share a time in your life when your mind, body and spirit felt fulfilled at the same time.
- share a youthful memory of something you enjoyed doing outdoors.
- describe a favorite place where you like to be.
- what healthy role model would you most like to have a conversation with. What would you talk about?

Activities:
- include a walk in nature before or after circle.
- each person journals thoughts/feelings about self image. Pair up and create positive affirmations. Share affirmations in a circle round.
- draw two pictures: one of how you see yourself today and another of how you see yourself in the future.
- see Appreciation, Passing the Pulse and Art in the Activities section of the *Appendix*.

Closing the Circle:
- share any additional comments or insights gained from circle.
- share handouts, books that have been brought and any snacks.
- see suggestions under Opening.

Who Am I, Who Am I Becoming?

Gather in circle to celebrate each other - who you are and who you are becoming. Share stories about your hopes, passions, and joys. Listening to and sharing these stories deepens our connectedness and helps us to better know and appreciate others and ourselves. Together, we cast light on the possibilities before us.

Plan this circle with friends and/or family or as part of a group retreat. Create a supportive and relaxed atmosphere. If children are included, choose questions that are appropriate for their ages. See Family Night Circle or The Honoring Friendships Circle for additional ideas. If a potluck is planned, consider asking people to bring a favorite dish that expresses who they are or who they are becoming.

Under each of the following headings, there are several suggestions listed. Choose which are appropriate for your gathering; consider those participating and the time you have available.

Creating a Center:

The host and/or participants may provide the following items. Place these items in the center before the circle and/or during a circle round.

- items symbolic of transformation or change (examples: butterfly chrysalis, a packet of seeds, art or photographs depicting transformation or change in nature, people, cultures or the world)
- something that represents who you are or who you are becoming (favorite place, activity, interest)
- drawings, photographs or writings depicting who we are now and/or how we envision ourselves in the future
- writings about pivotal moments that led to transformation in our lives
- inspirational books about transformation or change

Choosing a Talking Piece:

- something symbolic of transformation or change (see examples under Creating Center)
- a small mirror symbolizing self reflection
- an item from nature (examples: a rock, flower, nest and eggs)
- the first person to speak chooses an item from those that have been placed in the center of the circle. It can be used as a talking piece until someone chooses something different.

Opening the Circle:

- light a candle with a dedication to honor the lessons that change brings to our lives and/or to honor those who help us deal with these changes.
- do a guided meditation. Author Shakti Gawain offers examples to use in many of her books including *Creative Visualization*.
- read a selection about acceptance, change or transformation.

Questions for Circle Rounds:
- introduce yourself and describe a favorite place, activity or interest and share what you like about it.
- what key words describe you now?
- what key words describe who you want to become or are becoming?
- recall a mentor or someone who has helped you make a change in your life.
- are you are risk taker? When?
- what inspires you?
- describe an important shift in your perspective. What led to the shift?
- share a turning point in your life and how it influenced who you are.
- if you could do anything, what would it be?
- if you could be any living thing, what would you be?
- if you could be an inanimate object, what would you be?
- if you could live anywhere in the world, where would it be?
- share a time in life that brought change or transformation.

Activities:
- The following are sentence completions: select the one/s you want to use, print on paper and hand out for people to complete and then share in a circle round.

  My life is guided by...

  I laugh when...

  Three things I like about myself are...

  I value...

  I appreciate...

  I would love to...

  I have always wanted to learn about...

  I am good at...

  I want to be better at...
- see Activities listed in A Retreat Circle.

Closing the Circle:
- share insights gained from circle.
- read an excerpt from a favorite book about change or transformation.
- play inspirational music.

Memories

Our memories are touchstones that we revisit throughout our lives. They bring forth a range of emotions and lessons to learn from. Reflecting on our experiences helps us understand ourselves and appreciate our relationships with others. This circle offers the opportunity to honor these experiences by sharing stories that hold special meaning for us.

Family and/or friends could join in this circle to share stories about favorite times, activities, places or special people in their lives. It is another circle that is enriched by having different ages and generations present. It is enlightening, for example, to hear how children's play has changed over time or how technology has changed our lives.

Memories can take us to places of great joy but also regret and loss. Be aware of this when planning this circle. This circle is not an appropriate place to deal with memories that have caused pain and remain difficult to revisit.

Consider having a potluck meal before or after circle. This provides more informal time to connect and share stories. Under each of the following headings, there are several suggestions listed. Choose which are appropriate for your gathering; consider those participating and the time you have available.

Creating a Center:

The host and/or participants may provide the following items. Place these items in the center before the circle and/or during a circle round.

- handmade items from fabric, wood or other materials
- a valued item brought by each person
- flowers, a candle, items from nature
- favorite photos
- a precious item from your grandparents
- handouts of a poem or reading to be shared
- candy, home baked delicacies or a beverage to be shared

Choosing a Talking Piece:

- an heirloom
- an item chosen for its special memories
- an inspirational symbol
- a long stemmed flower
- a spiritual book

Opening the Circle:

- have a brief moment of silence.
- do breath work or stretching.
- dedicate a candle to honor the collective memories of those present.
- read a poem or a favorite passage from a book.
- play music chosen for its special meaning.

Questions for Circle Rounds:
- introduce yourself and share a recent blessing.
- share the story of any items brought for the center of the circle.
- share a story around a central theme (examples: a favorite activity, a special place, tradition or a favorite food and how it was prepared).
- honor a mentor/teacher by sharing her/his significance in your life.
- recall a favorite memory from your childhood/teenage/young adult/middle age years.
- share how you have mentored someone in your life.
- share one of life's greatest blessings.
- tell about a funny moment in life.
- what has been one of your favorite times in life?
- what is one lesson you wish you could teach other generations?

Activities:
- see Appreciation, A Gift Sharing, Sharing Values and Art described in the Activities section of the *Appendix*.

Closing the Circle:
- read an inspirational passage, poem or letter.
- each person reflects on the meaning the circle had for her/him.
- sing a song from a special time period or event.
- share treats and/or a beverage.

Life Celebration

A Life Celebration Circle honors a person at any stage of life or can be planned for someone who has passed on. In this circle we share stories about a person's life or focus on a specific topic such as the gifts or lessons she/he has given to us.

This circle is a gift to everyone present. It creates a space that allows expressions that otherwise might not be shared. The circle is also an opportunity for the person honored to offer thanks to others for their support.

Include family members and friends in planning, and if possible, the person being honored. Ask what would be a meaningful setting, who they would like present, if they would like to do an opening or closing or bring a talking piece. Include different generations to create a gathering rich in stories.

Under each of the following headings, there are several suggestions listed. Choose which are appropriate for your gathering; consider those participating and the time you have available.

Creating a Center:

The host and/or participants may provide the following items. Place these items in the center before the circle and/or during a circle round.

- a candle/s
- items representing the interests, values or accomplishments of the person
- writings from each person reflecting the significance of the life being honored
- life history in photographs
- gifts/tokens

Choosing a Talking Piece:

- a valued item of the person being honored
- a symbol of faith
- a small book of spiritual writings
- a small picture of the person being honored

Opening the Circle:

- light a candle to honor our shared journey in life.
- relate a special story or memory of the person being honored.
- share an inspirational reading or poem.

Questions for Circle Rounds:

- introduce yourself and share how you know/knew the person being honored.
- share the story of any items brought for the center of the circle.
- offer a blessing and light a candle - place it in the center.
- share a story or funny memory about this person.
- what is a valuable lesson you have learned from her/him?

- what have you most enjoyed about her/him?
- what gifts have you received from her/him?
- what is one thing you would like this person to know that you have not expressed?

Activities:
- see Appreciation, A Gift Sharing, Sharing Values, Celebration Wreath, Wall of Memories and Art (create a collage of memories surrounding her/his life) listed under Activities in the *Appendix.*

Closing the Circle:
- present an inspirational reading.
- each person shares well wishes for the honoree.
- place the honored person in the center and use hands to convey a "sprinkling" of love and blessings.

Universe

Space   Flowers

Animals   Rocks

Clouds   Trees

The World
Around Us

Garden   Earth

Desert   Sky

Moon   Stars

People

Spring Celebration Story

Jodi's Story

"I won't be home Wednesday night," I told my husband when receiving an invitation for a Spring Celebration Circle. I had wanted to experience circle for the past year and wasn't going to miss it! But Wednesday night arrived and my mind was exhausted from the previous few days of contemplation about making a huge shift in my life. "Should I or shouldn't I go" ran back and forth in my head like a stuck tape recorder. Maybe I would break down, fall apart - I really didn't know what to expect. And how would the other women perceive me? It didn't matter. I needed this night. Something deep within me said, "Go!"

The weather that magical day in May reached an unusual 91 degrees. It was sunny with a soft breeze - just enough to enhance the sweet smell of spring. We gathered beside Long Pond around a campfire. The setting had always been a favorite spot for me. Our host Robin, and others that would be present, are dear souls, and their company would be therapeutic just by being in their presence.

Robin began circle by playing a Tibetan singing bowl that sent vibrations to my soul. I have never heard and felt anything like it before - the music was a gift in itself. We took turns lighting candles, one by one, as we passed the talking piece - a special rock that indicated our time and only our time to talk. Nature and places special to us were the topics of celebration and conversation for the evening - we shared stories about something in nature we felt close to. As I sat and listened with one ear as each woman shared her thoughts and memories, I listened with the other, mesmerized by all the nature around us; Canadian Geese, Cardinals, Loons, Wood Ducks, Chickadees, to name a few. I was moved by the stories that were shared in circle.

As we said our goodbys and parted after we walked along the swampy woods, I couldn't help but look up and stare at the moon, listen to the frogs and ponder about the cycle of life and death. Maybe the reason we are here is to discover the mystery of life. Something had happened that night at circle. All the tugging and pulling that had been going on in my mind had stopped. And a sense of peace filled my soul.

The next morning brought excitement, courage and a stronger vision. The decision I struggled with the past few months, even years, became clear. I now had the strength to decide my future. I was given a gift of creativity along with the love for nature - I had forgotten it was such a big part of who I am. With the spring breeze and the unity of that night, it all seemed to come together!

Author's Note

Outdoors, around a campfire, where we can hear and feel the presence of nature, is a great place to hold a circle. The talking piece can be something from earth – a rock as was used in this circle, wood, flowers, a packet of seeds, a corn cob – anything that may be near the place you are holding circle. Some circles have participants write an answer to a reflective question and submit to the fire as a meaningful ritual. Simply sharing our individual stories about the gifts of nature makes for a meaningful gathering.

Planning an outdoor circle around the time of a full moon brings light and shadows and can add to the beauty of an evening circle. Drumming, singing, or any other way creating sound together brings unity of spirit outdoors.

There is something about nature and all its wonderment that helps settle our minds and balances and restores us. It did just that for Jodi, who was looking for answers in her life.

Special Places

A special place in our life provides us comfort and joy. Think about where this is for you. It might be a favorite outdoor area, a quiet place to read, a vacation retreat, a place with spiritual meaning, or even the presence of a special person. For some, this place is simply a state of well-being or a space created in the imagination. Wherever our special place exists, we are drawn there by the gifts it offers: relaxation, reflection, and renewal.

This circle helps us explore why we are drawn to a special place and gives us the opportunity to celebrate what it brings into our lives. A setting outdoors, around a campfire, or in a garden are wonderful places to hold this circle, but a peaceful indoor setting also works well. Consider bringing together family and/or friends of different ages to share the special places in their lives.

Under each of the following headings, there are several suggestions listed. Choose which are appropriate for your gathering; consider those participating and the time you have available.

Creating a Center:
The host and/or participants may provide the following items. Place these items in the center before the circle and/or during a circle round.

- items representing special places in our lives (examples: photographs of a place or something from nature)
- a candle and flowers placed on a favorite cloth
- readings about special places and their meaning in our lives

Choosing a Talking Piece:
- something symbolic of the meaning of place (example: comfort, peace, inspiration, fun, challenge, excitement, reflection)
- an item chosen from those that have been placed in the center of the circle

Opening the Circle:
- share a reading that captures the power of special places.
- play or perform music that captures the feeling or significance of a special place.
- lead a guided meditation.

Questions for Circle Rounds:
- introduce yourself and share a memory from childhood of a special place.
- share the story of any items brought for the center of the circle
- describe a special place in your life. What draws you there?
- how do you feel when you are there? What does it mean to you?
- do you share this place with others? If so, how?
- describe special places in your everyday life.
- describe a place you would like to explore.

Activities:
- see Word Reflection (on the phrase "special place") listed under Activities in the *Appendix*.

Closing the Circle:
- each person shares insights gained from the circle and parting thoughts.
- see suggestions under Opening.

Celebrating Nature

Many of us have childhood memories and experiences of exploring and enjoying nature. Even in the city, the trees in a park can feel like a large woods to a small child. Our memories are often a combination of adventure, fun, sometimes fear, and for some, spiritual connection. A nature circle focuses our attention on places, animals, and all that exists in the natural world around us.

In this circle people relate experiences about the importance of nature in their lives and the gifts it offers. Each person is invited to share what has special meaning for her/him such as rocks, lakes, trees, the prairie, or animals. The circle might also focus on one theme such as "a special place in nature." The choices are unlimited. Include children or several generations to get a glimpse of how our connection to nature has changed and yet stayed the same over time.

As all circles, this one could be held in a variety of settings. See the "Spring Celebration Story" at the beginning of this section for a description of a nature circle.

Under each of the following headings, there are several suggestions listed. Choose which are appropriate for your gathering; consider those participating and the time you have available.

Creating a Center:
The host and/or participants may provide the following items. Place these items in the center before the circle and/or during a circle round.
- valued items from nature such as a branch, nest, pine cone or shell
- fresh-picked flowers
- a collection of stones
- representations of animals such as a toy stuffed or ceramic lion or turtle
- candles in various shapes such as animals, leaves or rocks
- favorite books about nature
- a small water fountain

Choosing a Talking Piece:
- a natural item such as a rock, bone, piece of wood, pine cone, leaf, flower or a nest
- a toy stuffed animal
- a photo of a special place or something in nature
- a small globe
- a vial of pond/lake/ocean water

Opening the Circle:
- share a reading about the natural world.
- play taped sounds from nature.
- have a moment of silence, with the sound of a water fountain in the background.

Questions for Circle Rounds:
- participants introduce themselves through something they relate to in nature such as a flower or rock.
- tell the story about any items brought for the center of the circle.
- share a gift of something you have learned from nature.
- if you could be any living thing in nature, what would it be? Why?
- if you could be any inanimate object in nature, what would it be? Why?
- share a childhood memory about nature.
- share something you have always wondered about in nature.
- read excerpts from a favorite book about nature.
- explore ways to protect and care for nature.

Activities:
- sit outside and listen for all the sounds you can hear. Write these down and share in circle. Notice which sounds you are drawn to. This activity increases our awareness of our surroundings.
- before the circle, ask those interested to explore how an area (neighborhood, city, river) has changed through time. Share observations and relevant photographs as a circle round.

Closing the Circle:
- each person shares insights from the circle.
- play recorded bird songs or any sounds that capture the feeling of nature.
- imitate bird calls.

Culture and Tradition

This circle is an opportunity to increase our awareness and understanding of other cultures, religions, or traditions. Appreciating the diversity of people around us is the inspiration for planning this gathering. You can celebrate the culture of a particular group or the many cultures represented among those attending. This is a circle that benefits from including children and different generations. This circle becomes a time capsule of how cultures and traditions influence our lives and change over time.

The setting can be a home, church, or cultural center. A potluck meal with traditional foods from each culture will add to the fun and flavor of the event.

Under each of the following headings, there are several suggestions listed. Choose which are appropriate for your gathering; consider those participating and the time you have available.

Creating a Center:

The host and/or participants may provide the following items. Place these items in the center before the circle and/or during a circle round.

- items representing a particular culture, religion or tradition
- intergenerational pictures
- a traditional or antique family vase filled with flowers
- cultural heirlooms
- participants' written reflections of their culture, religion or tradition
- diaries, traditional stories and/or family genealogy

Choose a Talking Piece:

- an item symbolic of what is valued about a culture, religion or tradition
- a miniature replica of a person clothed in native dress
- a small heirloom
- a coin from a native country

Opening the Circle:

- share music, story or art representative of the culture, religion or tradition.
- share a reading or words from an elder or honored guest.
- play traditional music or have a dancer perform a cultural dance.
- share a traditional saying, poem or prayer.
- make a candle dedication to honor those who have passed on.

Questions for Circle Rounds:

- introduce yourself and share something about your favorite tradition.
- share the story of any items brought for the center of the circle.
- share something you value about your culture, religion or tradition.
- share a story about how your views about other cultures or religions have changed.

- tell a special story about a valued elder.
- what traditions does your family have?
- what traditions would you like to bring into your life and family?
- relate something important you have learned from another culture.
- what questions do you have about other cultures?

Activities:
- see Art listed under Activities in the *Appendix*.

Closing the Circle:
- each person relates something she/he learned in the circle
- participants share a culture they would like to learn more about.
- see suggestions under Opening.

Winter/Summer Solstice

The word solstice comes from the Latin sol stetit, meaning "sun stands still," which it does twice a year for six days: once in June and again in December. The 21st of June marks the Summer Solstice and December 21st the Winter Solstice.

Indigenous cultures honored the Summer and Winter Solstice as a sacred event and today many societies are carrying on this tradition. A circle offers a meaningful way to gather for this event.

John Matthews, in his book *The Winter Solstice*, writes the month of December is a time of letting go of old thoughts, ideas, and things that no longer serve us. It is also the time to think about what we want to invite into our lives with the coming of the New Year.

Celebrating the solstice reminds us of the gifts nature provides and offers us an opportunity to express our appreciation for them. The sun warms our earth and brings energy and light, increased activity, and the growth of plants that sustain us throughout the year. In the winter the sun retreats, making shorter days and providing more time for introspection. Honoring the Summer and Winter Solstice awakens our awareness of the sun's cycles and our interdependence with nature.

Under each of the following headings, there are several suggestions listed. Choose which are appropriate for your gathering; consider those participating and the time you have available.

Creating a Center:
The host and/or participants may provide the following items. Place these items in the center before the circle and/or during a circle round.
- a cloth with the earth's or sun's colors: green, blue, red or bright yellow
- a ceramic or metal sun
- items from nature: vines, a nest, pine cones or shells
- fresh picked flowers in a mason jar (Summer Solstice)
- springs of holly, ivy and mistletoe (Winter Solstice)
- bowls of grains, seeds, fruit or vegetables
- a candle/s in colors or shapes of the season

Choosing a Talking Piece:
- a symbol of the sun
- an item from nature such as a rock, piece of wood, pine cone, a small plant or a nest
- photo of a place or item in nature
- a small snow globe (Winter Solstice)
- a packet of grass or flower seeds (Summer Solstice)

Opening the Circle:
- read a selection that honors the beauty of nature.
- offer a candle dedication honoring the energy, warmth and light the sun

brings to us.
- play sounds from nature.
- play chimes or a Tibetan singing bowl.
- start the circle outside; form a circle around a tree and share a word that expresses your feeling about nature.

Questions for Circle Rounds:
- introduce yourself through something in nature that you connect with.
- share the story of any items brought for the center of the circle.
- light a candle to honor something you love in nature and place it in the center.
- what is a gift you have received from nature?
- what gifts do you receive from the summer and winter seasons?
- how does the light of the sun influence your life?
- what is your favorite season? Why?
- recall a happy time you spent in nature as a child.
- what does the long night/darkness mean to you?
- recall something you have learned about or from nature.
- what are some old thoughts, ideas or things that you would like to leave behind as you enter the New Year?
- what are some things you would like to invite into your life with the New Year?
- what traditions does your family have this time of year?
- what traditions would you like to instill in your family?

Activities:
- make suns or snowflakes with construction paper. Write your wishes for the season, fold them and place them in center.
- outside, each participant finds something in nature they are drawn to. Back in circle, they describe what the item reflects to them and presents it to the person on their left.
- refer to *The Winter Solstice: The Sacred Traditions of Christmas* by John and Caitlin Matthews. The book contains ideas for recipes, activities, ceremony and celebration.
- see Art and Writing (word reflection on sun, season, nature) listed under Activities in the *Appendix*.

Closing the Circle:
- play recorded sounds from nature (example: bird songs, sounds from the ocean).
- share an inspirational reading.
- participants blow out candles as they share their closing thoughts and reflections of the circle.

Earth Day

Earth day is observed on April 22 of every year. Holding a circle to commemorate this special event raises an awareness of how we care for our earth and the many ways it provides for us. It offers us the opportunity to express gratitude for the resources we so freely use and helps us appreciate the contributions we make in caring for our earth.

To care for the earth, we need to feel a personal connection to it. Planting a tree or flowers, a quiet walk in the woods, or canoeing personalizes nature for us. These interactions with the earth create a desire to protect it so we may continue to enjoy its wonder.

The setting for this circle could be in a yard or park or indoors where there are ample windows to view nature. It could also be held in a classroom as a way for students to learn how to care for our earth. An earth-based business might host circles on this day for the public or their work staff.

A circle could come at the close of a workday after planting trees or a garden in the community, cleaning up the neighborhood, or picking up trash in the ditches of our highways. This circle also expands and deepens the experience of working together.

Under each of the following headings, there are several suggestions listed. Choose which are appropriate for your gathering; consider those participating and the time you have available.

Creating a Center:
The host and/or participants may provide the following items. Place these items in the center before the circle and/or during a circle round.
- fabric or cloth in earth colors
- a stick, feather or pine cone
- freshly picked flowers
- a bowl of stones
- tree or shrub seedlings
- natural items people are drawn to

Choosing a Talking Piece:
- an item from nature such as a rock, piece of wood or pine cone
- a seedling or packet of seeds
- a miniature globe

Opening the Circle:
- share a reading from *Earth Prayers From Around the World* by Elizabeth Roberts and Elias Amidon or other publications that offer writings about honoring the earth. Native American authors are a wonderful resource.
- make a candle dedication to honor the earth and its gifts to us.
- play taped sounds from nature.

- start the circle outside; form a circle around a tree and share words honoring nature.

Questions for Circle Rounds:
- introduce yourself and share a place in nature you enjoy.
- share the story of the item in nature you are drawn to, share why and place it in the center.
- what are the gifts you have received from nature?
- what is your favorite outside activity?
- what is something you have you learned about nature?
- recall one of your favorite memories outdoors as a child.
- what is something you have always wondered about in nature?
- what is one thing that you do to care for the environment?
- what is one thing you would like to do for the environment?

Activities:
- see Art Activities under Activities in the *Appendix.*
- plant or restore an area.
- outside, each participant finds something in nature they are drawn to. Back in circle, describe what that item reflects to them and then present it to the person on the left.
- plan or participate in a bird count.
- brainstorm projects the group might want to do to care for the community.

Closing the Circle:
- share hopes for the environment.
- present a reading about the importance of nature and preserving it.
- play music that captures the sounds and feelings of nature.
- share a blessing for the trees, flowers, the sky and the universe.
- sit in silence and just listen and then share what you heard.

Peace

All of us are seekers of peace. Whether it is a quiet moment, a new understanding, an end to war, or simply a friendly exchange, we yearn for a more peaceful world. A Peace Circle invites us to recognize and celebrate the offerings of peace we give and receive in our homes, communities, workplace, and world. By doing so, we honor and expand our capacity as peacemakers.

This circle gives people of different ages and life experiences a way to share their views of peace and how it is a part of their lives. It might include family, friends, and a youth or community group.

Under each of the following headings, there are several suggestions listed. Choose which are appropriate for your gathering; consider those participating and the time you have available.

Creating a Center:

The host and/or participants may provide the following items. Place these items in the center before the circle and/or during a circle round.

- symbols representing the meaning, values, feelings or hopes of peace
- items that capture the spirit of peace such as photographs of a special person, place or event
- books and writings on peace

Choosing a Talking Piece:

- a peace symbol
- candles/flowers
- a globe
- something from nature representing the interconnectedness of all things
- an item chosen from those placed in the center

Opening the Circle:

- share quotes about peace such as "Peace around us and peace within us are intimately related to one another." from *The Courage for Peace* by Louise Diamond. See other sources by Gandhi, Martin Luther King or *The Practice of Peace* by Harrison Owen.
- offer a candle dedication to peace.
- share an inspirational reading or prayer about peace (example: "To put an end to outward war, you must put an end to war in yourself." J. Krishnamurri, *The First and Last Freedom*.)
- read excerpts from wartime letters, books or poems.
- play music reflecting peace.

Questions for Circle Rounds:

- introduce yourself, light a candle for the center and share what peace means to you.

- share the story of any items brought for the center of the circle.
- what brings you peace?
- describe a person in your life who has taught you a valued lesson about peace?
- what are the strengths you value in a peacemaker?
- when or where do you feel most peaceful?
- what promotes understanding among people within a family/community/ world?
- share a story from your life about peace.
- what are the challenges to peacemaking? Share a time when you overcame such a challenge.
- describe a strength you bring to peacemaking.
- what are your hopes and visions for peace in your life, community, country and/or world?

Activities:
- plan a word reflection on the word peace. See Word Reflection under Activities in the *Appendix*.
- Brainstorm one way the group could contribute to peacemaking.

Closing the Circle:
- share parting thoughts.
- share a simple circle dance or song.
- see suggestions under Opening.

Circles In Other Settings

People are expanding the application of circles by using them for celebrating, sharing information, gaining understanding, and building community. They are found internationally, in organizations, communities, schools, families, and even cyberspace.

An example of circles used internationally is Palden Jenkin's work dedicated to alleviating world crises. In 1995 he held a circle with the focus on nuclear testing with Bosnia, Israel, Nigeria, China, and France. Christina Baldwin and Ann Linnea, of PeerSpirit, Inc., bring circle into mainstream culture by offering practicums and wilderness adventures for organizations and individuals.

Peacemaking Circles, a partnership between volunteers of the community and government, provide a holistic response to crime and have been used by Native American and other cultures for many years. These circles are part of a growing restorative justice initiative to help communities address crime and violence. See *Peacemaking Circles: From Crime to Community* by Pranis, Stuart and Wedge listed under Circle Resources, Books for Learning More About Circles.

Jack Zimmerman along with Ruthann Saphier and Maureen Murdock introduced the circle, or council-based, "Mysteries Program" at Crossroads School in Santa Monica, California, to provide a community setting where students' issues can be discussed. In other classrooms across the country, students sit in a circle to plan and share experiences. Heartland Inc., founded in 1995 by Craig and Patricia Neal, uses the circle format to convene conversations, programs, trainings, and communities of engagement, dedicated to creating a world that works for all. They state that knowing how we do is as important as what we do - we convene conversations and gatherings to practice the skills of the new leader.

There are many other kinds of circles such as legacy and drumming circles. Circle is even on the worldwide web. Peter and Trudy Johnson-Lenz have created a virtual circle offering web participants the circle experience! Circle is everywhere and finding its way into the fabric of our lives.

Schools and Youth Groups

Circle can be used in a school setting by classmates, teachers, youth or sport groups, the staff and administration. Sitting in a circle, at the same level, creates a space for students to comfortably learn how to present and express themselves. Using a talking piece slows conversation, allows one person to speak at a time, teaches participants to truly listen, and gives them time to process what is being said. Within a school setting, the focus of a circle can be to:
- "show and tell"
- share what is learned from doing a project
- share a favorite classroom activity
- present information and get feedback from students
- introduce and welcome a new student or staff member
- honor an accomplishment
- celebrate birthdays
- explore ways to improve learning
- share creative work
- honor a teacher
- generate new ideas
- open or close each day or week of class
- share what has been learned from each other

An example of a how a circle was used for a presentation to a first grade class is The Green Sea Turtles earlier in the book. The circle provided a tool for learning and getting feedback from students. Refer to the Circle Theme section for circles that may apply to a school setting or the following two circles we created. The book *Kidchat: Questions to Fuel Young Minds and Mouths* provides wonderful questions for youth circles. The following two examples are circles that can be used for school and youth groups:

Youth Circle

A world that cares for its youth spreads hope and possibility. This circle brings youth into a safe setting where their stories and ideas can be heard. Too often we talk to youth instead of with them. This space creates a place for them to voice their thoughts, explore questions, and have a respectful dialogue about a variety of topics such as goals, interests, sources of inspiration, or ideas on dealing with conflict effectively. Consider what topics are appropriate and help guide the dialogue so that the space is kept respectful and inclusive.

Those participating can be of different ages, points of view, and cultures. If someone with a particular experience or skill is invited to be part of the youth circle to share their story, make sure everyone also has an opportunity to share her/his views and experiences.

Settings for this circle could be any place where youth typically meet such as a community center, at school, church, or someone's home. A Youth Circle can be held on its own or as a part of a gathering or group outing. You may choose to include a formal opening and closing or simply use a question or two such as those listed under Circle Rounds for an informal circle. Refer to other circles for additional questions that may be suitable for your group.

Under each of the following headings, there are several suggestions listed. Choose which are appropriate for your gathering; consider the number participating and the time you have available.

Creating a Center:

The host and/or participants may provide the following items. Place these items in the center before the circle and/or during a circle round.

- items representing the group's identity:
- items symbolic of the circle topic: (example: the topic of "What or Who Has Inspired You" - pictures of a person who has been inspirational, an inspirational book or art piece or a religious/spiritual piece)
- photographs of the group or individual pictures pertaining to the focus of circle

Choosing a Talking Piece:

- a small item of value brought by a participant
- an item made collectively before circle
- something representing the focus of circle (example: if the topic is gratitude, an item representing something they are grateful for)

Opening the Circle:

- read a passage that relates to the focus of circle.
- play a short musical selection.
- give a brief dramatic presentation.
- light a candle and make a dedication (example: to a person valued by the group).

Questions for Circle Rounds:

- introduce yourself and share something you have done recently that has brought you happiness.
- share any stories of items brought for the center.
- what is one thing you are thankful for?
- describe a person you admire or who has influenced you.
- what inspires you?

- describe a favorite book, movie, play music, art or activity and how it has influenced you.
- relate how you have dealt with conflict in a good way.
- what is something you would like to learn or know more about?
- share a goal you would like to set for yourself.
- describe a favorite place and what it means to you.
- describe a favorite activity and what it means to you.
- where do you think wisdom comes from?
- see other circles such as Wisdom, Gratitude, What you are Drawn To, Family night and Honoring Friends for other circle round suggestions.

Activities:
- see Word Reflection in the Activities section of the *Appendix*. (Examples for words to use: inspiration, teamwork, discovery, exploration, learning.)
- include a walk in nature before or after circle.
- participants draw a picture of how they see themselves today and how they would like to see themselves in the future.
- see the Activities section in the *Appendix* for other ideas.

Closing the Circle:
- share your thoughts or something you have gained from circle.
- see suggestions under Opening.

Getting to Know Each Other

Hold this circle to welcome a new student or for the students and teachers to get to know each other better. Under each of the following headings, there are several suggestions listed. Choose which are appropriate for your gathering; consider those participating and the time you have available.

Creating a Center:
- a patchwork, paper "rug" made by students with construction paper and art supplies (Examples: each student does a patch reflecting their favorite things.)
- items or photographs brought by each student that reflect a favorite activity, interest or cultural value or tradition

Choosing a Talking Piece:
- an item from nature (a stone, feather or pine cone)
- an item brought or made by a student or group of students
- a paper crown to wear rather than a talking piece to hold

Opening the Circle:
- music or sounds from a chime or symbol
- introduction about the focus of the circle by a student or teacher

- sing a song together
- a word game

Questions for Circle Rounds:
- introduce yourself and respond to a question the teacher asks such as one below.
- share the story of any items brought for the center of the circle.
- what is your favorite thing to do?
- what is one of the best things that happened today (the weekend)?
- what is your favorite book? Why?
- what is your favorite animal?
- what animal do you think you are most like? Why?
- who is one of your favorite people? Why?
- bring a picture of your family and tell us about them.

Activities:
- see Art Activities and A Gift for All, listed under Activities in the *Appendix*.

Closing the Circle:
- sing a song together.
- each students shares something she/he learned from the circle.
- share a reading in unison.

Workplace and Community Organizations

People in organizations and businesses are exploring and discovering ways to effectively use the circle process. Increasingly, the importance of building relationships and appreciating each person's strengths and contributions is being valued. Participating in a circle process helps revitalize energies by creating a space that provides an opportunity to listen and learn from each other. How and when the circle is used depends upon the goals, values and culture of an organization. Circles within the workplace or an organization can be held to:

- share successes.
- share what each person values about the organization.
- document the history of the group.
- create a vision for the future.
- develop an understanding of an issue or event.
- highlight values and guiding principles of the organization.
- honor employees or volunteers for the gifts they bring to the organization.
- plan and brainstorm for ideas on issues.
- honor an individual's accomplishments, birthday, retirement, upcoming wedding or birth of a child (check *Circle Themes* for ideas).
- share life's stories.

Invite others to help plan the circle. Create a respectful space where each person has an opportunity to express their thoughts, be heard and have their ideas considered. The following is an example of a circle that could be held to honor a group of workers for their contribution to the organization:

Working Together Circle

Opportunities for learning how to work successfully with others are presented to us throughout our lives. At an early age, play introduces us to both the joys and challenges of group interaction. Growing up we learn that even competition requires cooperation. Our most valued work and volunteer efforts are often when collaborations result in shared accomplishments.

Much has been written about how to support cooperative and creative efforts. Both thrive best where there is support for a diversity of skills and experience, a shared mission that is valued, and opportunities for learning and exchanging information. The key is developing communication that strengthens connections among people and builds both individual and group capacities.

While a collaborative environment is more likely to support learning, creativity and personal investment in working towards shared goals, it is not always easy to create and sustain. The joys that come from successfully working with others are many including an environment that is more creative, supportive, and productive. In this circle, participants learn from each other by drawing on life experiences about what contributes to cooperative efforts. Sharing these insights can help groups gain a deeper understanding of how to effectively work together.

Under each of the following headings, there are several suggestions listed. Choose which are appropriate for your gathering; consider those participating and the time you have available.

Creating a Center:

Determine if creating a center for your circle is appropriate for your setting. If so, the host and/or participants may provide the following items. These items may be placed in the center before the circle and/or during a circle round. Consider the setting and those involved as to which of the following is appropriate:
- items that represent being part of a team effort
- mission or vision statements
- photographs or products of cooperative efforts

Choosing a Talking Piece:
- an item symbolic of an important value, goal or accomplishment

Opening the Circle:
- an excerpt from an important report, mission statement or history
- quotes from clients about what they value about the organization
- a reading about cooperation or team building

Questions for Circle Rounds:
- introduce yourself and share what the word "cooperation" means to you.
- share the story of any items brought for the center.
- on a piece of 4x6 paper or a paper plate, write a value or action that contributes to cooperation; share why it is important and place in the center.
- relate a story about a time when people successfully worked together. What did you do? What did others do? What did you learn about cooperation and what supports it?
- share how you contribute to cooperative efforts.
- what are the challenges to cooperation? How would you address these?
- what does cooperation look like? How does it feel?
- how can you and the organization support collaborative efforts?
- how do collaboration and creativity support each other?

Activities:
- word reflection on the word "cooperation." Do a Word Reflection Activity in the *Appendix*.
- see Sharing Values Activity in the *Appendix*.

Closing the Circle:
- each person shares final observations and thoughts about the circle.
- see suggestions under Opening

Appendix

Suggested Circle Activities

Appreciation

Provide a sheet of paper and a pen or pencil for each person. Place your name at the top and pass the paper to the person on your left. The person receiving the paper with your name writes a positive observation about you and passes it on to the next person. This continues until everyone has written something about each person in the circle. The paper with your name comes back to you after participants complete their comments. Invite participants to share what was written about them.

If honoring a specific person/s, give an index card to each participant. Ask them to write a few words describing the gifts of this person/s. Each person reads her/his card and presents it as a gift. From *Sacred Circles: A Guide to Creating Your Own Women's Spirituality Group* by Robin Deen and Sally Craig.

A Gift Sharing

Ask participants to bring a small gift, wrapped or unwrapped, such as a poem, rock, a book or something that has special meaning that they are willing to give away. At the beginning of the circle, these are placed in the center. At the closing, each person in circle chooses one item. The first person to choose could be the one being honored, the oldest or youngest, or the person who traveled the farthest. After an item is chosen, the person who brought it shares its significance and then becomes the next person to choose a gift.

Celebration Wreath

Meg Cox, in *In the Heart of a Family*, describes an activity to use as part of a birthday celebration or adapted for other circle celebrations. The wreath becomes a meaningful gift and a memory of the circle. Invite participants to bring a small item representing something significant about the person being honored. The wreath can be made from a variety of materials. During or at the close of the circle, attach items brought by participants to the wreath and present it as a reminder of the celebration circle.

Candle Wishes

Place a cake and one large candle on a base in the center of the circle. Pass a container of small cake candles around the circle and have each person take one. Ask one person to light the large candle in the center and make a wish for the honoree. One by one have each participant light her/his candle from the center candle, make a wish and place it in the cake. This could be part of a variety of circles such as Birthday, Shower or Retirement.

Wall of Memories

Choose a blank wall space for the activity. As people in circle share memories, write them on a sheet of paper or 5 x 7 cards and place them on the wall. If a family or specific group is represented in the circle, you may want to title the wall for example, the Smith's Wall of Memories. An example of questions for people to respond to are:

- a time you connected with someone in a new way
- a valued memory of a person or event
- a valued lesson from someone within the group
- an example of how someone was a mentor for you

The Wall of Memories may be copied and shared as part of documenting the history of a family, neighborhood, business, community, classroom or organization.

Art

- Before circle, invite one or several participants to create a talking piece that will be used.
- Collages: each participant creates a collage on tag board and shares what their creation represents during a circle round. For example: each person could make a collage representing who they are, things they like or places they want to go. Participants could also work together to create one collage on a particular theme such as wisdom or discovery. Provide tag board, magazines and art supplies.
- Painting Circle: each person starts painting or drawing a picture and then, after 10 minutes, she/he switches and passes it to the person on the left until everyone has added a bit to everyone else's. Submitted by Jessica Brumm in the *Blue Mountain* publication, Autumn 2004, Volume 15, Number 3.
- Create Pictures: use paints, crayons or pencils to create a picture that expresses something significant about the purpose of gathering. For example, each person draws a picture of how they see themselves today or in the future. Share in circle.

Writing

- Word Reflection: The words we use carry many different meanings. Sharing these helps us better understand ourselves and those around us. Choose one word that is relevant to the purpose of the circle. For example, gratitude, friendship, or beginnings. Ask everyone to take a few minutes to write down the different meanings the word carries. In the first circle round, ask participants to share what they wrote. In a second round, share insights gained from listening to the various meanings of the word. This activity is adapted from a word reflection developed at The Prospect Center, N. Bennington,

Vermont. An option to offer participants: draw or paint a picture reflecting the meaning of the word.

- A variation of the Word Reflection: pass a bowl containing cards with a word written on each card. Each person chooses a card, writes thoughts about the word and is invited to share her/his reflections with the group. Drake and Tyler have published Angel Cards with individual words such as joy, comfort, honesty, humor, and strength or you can create cards with words that hold meaning for your circle theme. An option to offer participants: draw or paint a picture reflecting the meaning of the word they have chosen.

- Group Poem: create a group poem that can be given as a gift to the person being honored. For example, ask each person to write a sentence about what they value about the person and then adapt and combine these into a poem.

Sharing Values

Sharing values that are important to us strengthens connections and expands our understanding of each other. Ask participants to write a value that is important in their life on a piece of paper or a plain paper plate. As an initial round, each participant shares the meaning it holds and places it in the center. As the circle continues, these words provide a visual reminder of what is important to those present. Participants often refer back to these values in subsequent rounds. The words need to be written large enough to be seen by everyone after placed in the center. The materials needed are paper or paper plates and markers.

You Are Invited
to (guest)'s
Birthday Celebration Circle

June 13th at 2:00 p.m.

*****

Please bring a small item that reminds you of (guest)
to tell its story and place in the center of the circle
(example: photo, memento)

*****

Please do not bring gifts -
Your presence is the Gift

*****

Hosted By:

_____

Location _____

Please RSVP by _____ Phone #_____

Directions:

(printed on colored paper, folded and sealed with a sticker)

You are Invited to a Spring Celebration Circle

Wednesday, April 28th, 7:00 p.m.

"Climb the mountains and get their good tidings. Nature's peace will flow into you as sunshine flows into trees. The winds will blow their own freshness into you, and the storms their energy, while cares will drop off like autumn leaves." John Muir

Please bring a small item to place in the circle center that signifies something in nature you are drawn to.

Hosted by: _____

Address: _____

Please RSVP by April 26th

Phone: _____

Directions:

Weather permitting, we will gather around the fire by the pond so dress accordingly.

(printed on recycled paper with images of insects)

You are Invited to a "Once in a Blue Moon" Celebration Circle

Tuesday, August 10, 7:00 p.m.

When the Blue Moon occurs it is an ideal time to do something you have never done before, something that will allow you to spread your wings and grow. Do something to honor the feminine divine that the moon energy empowers.

Please bring a small item to place in the circle center that signifies something something in your life that brings you happiness.

Hosted by: _____

Address: _____

Please RSVP by April 26th

Phone: _____

Directions:

(printed on blue paper that featured the moon and stars)

Notes on Planning a Circle

Inspiration for a circle may come from ourselves, family, friends, associates, or from a need within the community. Circles can range from being a planned event to a spontaneous question posed to each person during a gathering of family or friends. Examples of a circle requiring prior planning would be one held for a birthday or wedding, welcoming someone to the community, exploring a shared interest, or reaching a milestone in life. A more spontaneous circle might be simply taking turns sharing favorite memories or responding to an insightful question when a group has already gathered.

Circles can have more than one focus. For example, we hosted a circle celebrating the birthday of two sisters and honored a third sister who had passed the previous year. Another time we began a circle with a house blessing for the host and also expressed our appreciation to a colleague for her work.

A circle gathering can be held on its own or as part of a larger celebration. An example of a circle being included in a larger celebration would be a small group at a family or class reunion gathering to share stories around a selected topic. The circle themes we created in this book are generally onetime gatherings but could evolve into several circles held over a period of time. For guidance on long-term circle gatherings see books for learning more about circles in the *Circle Resources* section.

Any way you create a circle gathering is the right way if it honors your purpose and the participants. Our suggestions are based on what we have experienced and are offered as a guide only. Explore your own creative ideas!

Hosting/Guiding a Circle

Circles may be planned by a host/s or with the help of those who will attend. While everyone attending shares in creating the circle space, one or two people can guide the circle by welcoming people, introducing the openings and closings, beginning the circle rounds and inviting participation.

Who and How Many to Invite

If the purpose of your circle is to honor an event in a person's life, ask for her/his help in determining the guest list to ensure a memorable celebration. When holding a circle that focuses on a common interest, consider who shares this interest and would enjoy exploring it with others. Those attending can be peers or from different age groups. Children bring a wonderful perspective to circle. Consider including them if appropriate for the circle you are planning.

The size of a circle gathering varies. We usually invite six to fifteen people but we have participated in circles with over twenty participants. One of the circle stories, "My 85th Birthday," describes a beautiful gathering where fifty-two people were present. Just remember the larger the group, the longer it takes for the talking piece to make a complete pass around the circle.

If someone is apprehensive about attending, we describe circle in this way: "Circle is storytelling - a way of sharing our experiences to celebrate and honor each other." Reading for the opening or closing, may help reduce their level of uncertainty.

Length of Time

The length of time for circle varies depending on the purpose for gathering. We have hosted circles for a day and a half retreat but have, more spontaneously, posed a single question for a circle round at a gathering. If preplanning a circle, people seem most receptive committing to a one to two hour time frame. If a circle is held within the workplace or an organization, even an hour allows time to celebrate an event. Allow extra time if a snack or meal is part of your plan.

A suggestion is to plan five minutes for opening, about three to four minutes for each person to speak in each round of the talking piece, and five minutes for closing. Example: If nine people are attending and you gather for ninety minutes, you will have time for three rounds of the talking piece plus the opening and closing. You may want to have one to two questions in reserve for additional rounds in case the circle moves more quickly than anticipated. If an activity is planned, run through it before circle to determine approximately how long it will take.

Involving Others

Once you determine the purpose of your circle, think about ways to involve participants in the planning. It will make the experience more meaningful for them. For example, invite participants to bring:
- a special cloth, flowers or a candle for the center
- something for the opening or the closing
- a talking piece
- an item with special significance related to the purpose of the circle; participants will be invited to share the story of the item and place it in the center.
- a candle, with a base, to light in honor of a person/event
- food for a snack or meal

When honoring a specific person or group, invite them to help in the planning. The following are questions you might ask them:
- who would you like to have present?
- where would be a meaningful place to hold the circle?
- would you like to choose something you value to use as a talking piece?
- would you like to plan an opening or closing?

Invitations

Invitations can be verbal, by e-mail, or a hand written or printed invitation. Include the following:
- the purpose of the circle
- date and time the circle will begin and end

- any items people are to bring for the center of the circle; for candles, request a base
- directions to the gathering
- a contact number to RSVP or for any questions
- prior to some circles, you may want to send people a key question to consider. For example, for a Discovery Circle the question might be, "What Are You Drawn To?"

If you have time to design a special invitation, consider using a collage of photos, children's art work or symbols representing the theme of your circle. Sample invitations are located in the *Appendix*.

Creating an Inviting Space

Consider the following when selecting and arranging a setting:
- what kind of space will enhance the purpose of the gathering?
- what size space will comfortably accommodate the number of participants?
- which works best for those attending: sitting on furniture or on the floor with pillows?
- will music help set the tone?
- what kind of talking piece will reflect the purpose of the gathering?
- how much ceremony should be included? Should a center be created?
- what can others bring that will help create the space?
- will a snack or meal be included? Where and how will it be served?

Circles can be held in a home, at a school, church, community room, in the workplace, or even at an outdoor setting on a patio or around a fire ring. When planning a circle in any setting, ensure that everyone can see each other by setting chairs in a symmetrical circle or by using a round table.

Opening the Circle

An opening helps us focus and be present as the circle begins. The host/s or anyone planning to come may be asked to choose and present one. There are many ways to open a circle: deep breathing, simple stretches, a reading, ringing of a bell, lighting a candle with a dedication, music, silence, spontaneous words, or any other creative idea. Consider what is appropriate for the setting and purpose of gathering. See each individual circle for examples of openings.

Creating the Circle and Center Pieces

The center is naturally created by the placement of chairs or pillows in a circle. It holds the collective energy of the group and is made more visible by placing items within it. These items may be a combination of things chosen by the host and those participating. Examples may include a low table or cloth with a candle, flowers, a gift to be presented, or anything that reflects the intent of gathering. Decide if the ceremony of placing items in the center is appropriate for the purpose and setting of the circle you are holding. Visualize the environment you want to create and use your imagination.

Choosing a Talking Piece

Choose a talking piece that reflects the purpose of the circle and can be easily handed from person to person. The host/s or anyone attending may be asked to provide it. If honoring a specific person or group, invite them to bring something significant to them. A young adult we honored brought a medal earned for a physical sport. In another circle, a male brought an empty shell and told how it represented his first hunting experience and the gratitude he felt for the man who had taught him hunting skills.

The talking piece can be something valued, crafted specifically for the circle, or a gift that is given to the person/s being honored at the beginning of the circle. For example, at Nancy's daughter's 21st birthday circle, an egg made of crystal and fiber optic materials was used. As an egg, it represented a new beginning and the natural and man-made materials symbolized the interdependence between nature and people.

A variation to having one talking piece is using items participants have brought and placed in the center during the first round. On the second round, the first person to speak can choose any item from the center that she/he feels connected to. It can be used as a talking piece until someone chooses something different.

Circle Rounds

During a circle round, the talking piece is passed around the circle so each person has an opportunity to speak. The number of rounds to plan depends on the time available and the number of people. We have found that two to three questions for rounds works best for a one and a half to two hour circle involving ten to twelve people. A useful guide is three to four minutes per person per question. Consider having one or two questions in reserve to use if you have more time than anticipated. Choose topics or questions for circle rounds related to your purpose for gathering. For example: "What are you most grateful for?" or "What is your favorite family tradition?" See individual circles for other ideas to use in circle rounds or in the books listed in the *Circle Resources* section.

Activities

Creative arts and activities can be part of a circle. They are a fun and an easy way for people to learn about themselves and relate to each other. Creating collages, expressive writing, or other creative activities reveal different parts of our nature. These activities can be done individually or in a group. Go through the activity to estimate how much time it will take. Include enough time for people to share their experiences in circle. Choose age appropriate activities. Resources for activities are in the *Appendix*.

Closing the Circle

A closing marks the end of the circle and helps people prepare to leave. Ideas for a closing are a reading, a round of the talking piece for participants to comment on their experience of the circle, or closing words from the host/s.

Recording Circle Memories

Recording your circle may keep people from fully participating so decide if recording your circle is appropriate and always ask the group's permission first. If you plan on recording, there are many ways to do it:

- capture memories in writing.
- create a special memory book with stories, photos or special messages.
- take photos before/after circle.
- take a few photographs during the circle (only if the focus of circle is a light-hearted one).
- make a collage from any of the above and frame it.
- create an audio or video tape.

Reminders and Things to Consider

- include others in planning and contributing to the circle.
- if needed, ask if everyone can be flexible about the time frame for circle.
- be sensitive to the level of ceremony or ritual that is appropriate for your group, particularly in the workplace and schools.
- gatherings that celebrate and honor people can be emotional; have tissues available.
- when possible, include children in the planning and choose age-appropriate questions and activities.

Notes on Holding a Circle

Preparing the Circle Space

Consider the purpose of the circle and the needs of those who are attending. Arrange chairs or pillows on the floor in a circle to allow everyone to be seen as they speak. Sitting at a round table could also work in settings such as the workplace or at a family gathering. If appropriate, create a relaxing space with background music or candles. Let the focus of the circle guide you in creating a welcoming space.

Welcoming Everyone

Once people are in a circle, welcome everyone and thank them for coming. Those new to circle may have some apprehension. This is a good time to address that. Assure them with words such as "It is natural to be uncertain about experiencing something new, but circle is simply a way of gathering where we take turns speaking and everyone else listens. It is based on an ancient way of gathering and is a way to create a space where we share our stories and experiences."

If circle will last a long time, remind everyone when the circle will end and decide if a break is needed. Ask if anyone needs to leave before the end of circle. If someone does, it is less disruptive knowing this at the beginning of the circle. Share bathroom locations and other relevant information. Ask the group if all phones can be turned off.

Sharing the Purpose of Gathering

The host and others involved in the planning share the reason for gathering. This brings participants' thoughts into the present and connects the group.

Opening the Circle:

The host or another circle participant gives the opening. It may consist of one or combination of the following: a simple breathing exercise, stretching, a reading or musical selection, spontaneous words, lighting a candle with a dedication, or any other offerings that helps the group relax and focus. The person who provides the opening may share the significance it has for her/him.

Group Agreements

Group agreements keep the circle a respectful place for expression. Though we usually do not use agreements in celebration circles honoring traditional events such as a birthday or baby shower, others circle gatherings may need to have them. The most important agreement for circles is confidentiality – what is said in circle stays in circle. The following are other examples the group may wish to consider: listen with kindness, share what you feel comfortable sharing; speak only for yourself; give everyone equal time (you may mention around three or four minutes); and be sensitive to others. These suggestions are among those found in *The Mysteries Source Book,* by R. Kessler, Ed., a book that addresses circles within schools.

Invite the group to suggest other agreements; it is a reminder of the part each of us plays in creating a respectful gathering.

Introducing the Talking Piece

A way to introduce the talking piece is to express how using it changes our communication when in a group of people. A suggestion for words you may want to use:

"When we gather with others, we usually have many conversations going at one time. In circle we communicate in a different way. We use a talking piece that is passed from person to person and only the person holding it speaks while everyone else listens. The talking piece slows the pace of conversation, helps us process what each person says and honors the speaker by listening attentively to her/him."

Let people know they may choose not to speak and simply pass it to the next person. Ask the person bringing the talking piece to share why it was chosen and the meaning it carries. The talking piece is commonly passed to the left, the "sun" direction, though some cultures pass it to the right or "earth" direction, according to Jack Zimmerman and Virginia Coyle in *The Way of Council*. After everyone has an opportunity to speak, ask if anyone wants the talking piece again for additional comments or, if the group agrees, the talking piece may be placed in the center for open exchange.

Circle Rounds

A round is one complete pass of the talking piece around the circle, giving each participant an opportunity to speak. Suggestions for Questions for Circle Rounds:

- introductions and responses to a question such as, "How do you know the person being honored?" or "Share a recent blessing." A good question is one that relates to the purpose of the gathering and starts the circle on a positive note. The host may respond first to set the tone and help people feel more comfortable.
- light a candle and offer a dedication.
- share the story of items brought for the circle. If items are forgotten, ask participants to describe what they had planned to bring.
- respond to circle round questions selected for the circle.
- share responses from an activity.
- share closing comments

Suggestions for circle rounds and activities are listed under individual *Circle Themes* and also under Books for Questions for Circle Rounds in the *Circle Resources* section.

Closing the Circle

The closing can be presented by the host/s or anyone present. It can be similar to an opening such as a reading, a question that invites final thoughts on the time together, or the presentation of gifts. An example of a question would be "What did you enjoy or gain from the circle?" If candles or other items were placed in the center, participants may remove them out at this time. The closing helps participants prepare for leaving the circle.

Reminders and Things to Consider

- if participants want time for open dialogue in a longer-held circle, the talking piece may be placed in the center after the main circle rounds. If this leads to only a few people talking, send the talking piece around the circle again and invite input from everyone.
- if someone is overwhelmed emotionally during the circle give the person space and time to move through the feeling and continue the circle.
- if you have used group agreements at the beginning of circle and they are not being respected, people can be gently reminded how to share in keeping the circle a welcome place for everyone.
- if an issue is brought up that carries unresolved feelings, acknowledge the issue and let the circle decide how to deal with it. The options are dealing with it immediately or offering support at another time.

Circle Resources

Books For Learning More About Circles

The Art and Heart of Drum Circles by Christine Stevens. Wisconsin: Hal Leonard Corporation, 2003. Christine gives us a detailed guide on how to create drum circles. Quotes from drum circle participants express the transformational power of taking part in them. A CD is included to help facilitate a drum circle.

Calling the Circle: The First and Future Culture by Christina Baldwin. New York: Bantam Books, 1994,1998. Christina Baldwin presents information on starting and maintaining circles and includes inspiring stories of those who have used circle in their lives. She introduces us to circle and invites us to embrace this way of gathering that fosters a different and more meaningful way of doing and being in our lives.

The Ceremonial Circle: Practice, Ritual, and Renewal for Personal and Community Healing by Sedonia Cahill & Joshua Halpern. New York: HarperCollins, 1990,1992. Now out of print but available used, Cahill and Halpern enlighten us with their knowledge of Native American ritual and shamanic practices and their use within ceremonial circles.

The Circle is Sacred: A Medicine Book for Women by Scout Lee, Ed. D. Oklahoma: Council Oak Books, 1994. Dr. Lee combines ancient wisdom and contemporary spirituality in her guide to women's ceremony. Her book highlights Native American ceremonial objects, honors the people who touched her life and empowers the female. Scout Lee co-authored another book titled the *Circle is Sacred* with Carol Ann Washburn, 2003.

The Circle Way by Manitonquat. New Hampshire: Story Stone Publishing, 1997. Manitonquat (Medicine Story) is an elder of the Assonet Wampanoag, a story teller, lecturer, counselor and teacher of counseling and spiritual ways in prisons and in native and non-native communities. He describes how to create effective circles and the many applications in which to use circle. Available through: Another Place Inc., 173 Merriam Hill Rd., Greenville, NH 03048.

The Little Book of Circle Processes: A New/old Approach to Peacemaking "The Little Book of Justice & Peace Building Series" by Kay Pranis. Intercourse, PA, Good Books, 2005. Pranis gives us an overview of Peacemaking Circles and how they can be used in different settings.

The Medicine Way: How to Live the Teachings of the Native American Medicine Wheel, A Shamanic Path to Self-Discovery by Kenneth Meadows. Boston: Element Books, 2002. Meadows takes us on a journey for personal development using the ancient shamanic truths of the American Indian. He offers great knowledge, exercises and activities for this journey in his handbook.

The Millionth Circle: How to Change Ourselves and The World by Jean Shinoda Bolen, MD. California, Conari Press, 1999. Bolen believes women's circles can change society from traditional patriarchal to non-hierarchical equality. In this succinct book she offers the tools and inspiration to create these circles and expand on ones already created.

The Mysteries Source Book by R. Kessler, Ed. California, Crossroads School, 1982-1990. Kessler has created a book to implement circles into the school environment to deal with students issues and provide them with a voice. This book serves as a guide as well as offering a rich composite of stories that confirm the need for circles in our schools.

Peacemaking Circles: From Crime to Community by Kay Pranis, Barry Stuart and Mark Wedge, Living Justice Press, 2003. This is a helpful resource for those interested in restorative justice. The experienced authors share stories and information about using community peacemaking circles for community justice.

Sacred Circles: A Guide To Creating Your Own Women's Spirituality Group by Robin Deen Carnes & Sally Craig. New York: HarperCollins, 1998. Carnes and Craig address spirituality and our need to express it. They provide an excellent guide to create on-going circles, include themes for gathering and relate stories from those who have been empowered through participating in circle.

The Way of Council by Jack Zimmerman and Virginia Coyle. Las Vegas: Bramble Books, 1996. Zimmerman and Coyle show us how circle creates an environment to speak and listen from the heart while providing a safe place for expression within family, school and organizations. Zimmerman's implementation of circles at Crossroads Schools in 1983 was the first of many. Adjunct: The Mysteries Source Book listed above.

Wisdom Circles: A Guide to Self-Discovery and Community Building in Small Groups by Charles Garfield, Cindy Spring and Sedonia Cahill. New York: Hyperion, 1999. These authors offer a wonderful guide for long term circles. They recall the healing power of circles, how they create genuine community and their ability to change and expand our perspective about self and humanity.

Women Circling the Earth: A Guide to Fostering Community, Healing and Empowerment by Beverly Engel. Florida, Health Communications, Inc., 2000. Engel describes what a circle is, relates a story of her own healing and cites the need for a new women's movement to celebrate the values and wisdom of females. She interviews women who do circle work, suggests ways to use circles and provides resources for us.

Women's Lives, Women's Legacies: Passing Your Beliefs and Blessings to Future Generations by Rachel Freed. Minnesota, Fairview Press, 2003. Freed describes in detail how to use legacy circles as a tool for creating spiritual and ethical wills, recording values, wisdom and what holds special meaning in our lives. The wills are a portrait of who we are and become valuable gifts to present and future generations.

Books for Opening and Closing Circle

Blue Mountain: A Spiritual Anthology Celebrating the Earth by F. Lynne Bachleda, Ed. Alabama: Menasa Ridge Press, 2000.

Choosing Happiness: Keys to a Joyful Life by Alexandra Stoddard. New York: HarperCollins, 2002.

A Grateful Heart: Daily Blessings for the Evening Meal from Buddha to the Beatles by M.J. Ryan, Ed. California: Conari Press, 2002.

A Guide for the Advanced Soul: A Book of Insight by Susan Hayward. Canada: Little, Brown, & Company, 2008.

Earth Prayers From Around the World: 365 Prayers, Poems, and Invocations for Honoring the Earth by Elizabeth Roberts & Elias Amidon, Eds. California: HarperSanFranciso, 1991.

Expect Miracles: Inspirational Stories of the Miraculous in Everyday Life by Mary Ellen. Berkeley, Canari Press, 1999.

A Guide for Grown-ups: Essential Wisdom from the Collected Works of Antoine de Saint-Exupery by Antoine de Saint-Exupery. Florida: Harcourt, Inc., 2002.

The Healing Earth: Nature's Medicine for the Troubled Soul by Philip Sutton Chard, Wisconsin, NorthWord Press, Inc., 1999.

Heartsongs by 11 year old Mattie J.T. Stepanek. New York: Hyperion, 2002.

I Hope You Dance by Mark D. Sanders and Tia Sillers. Nashville: Rutledge Hill Press, 2000. Includes a CD by Lee Ann Womack.

In The Heart of the Word: Thoughts, Stories and Prayers by Mother Theresa. California: New World Library, 1997.

Mysteries of Marriage: Meditations on the Miracle by Mike Mason. Oregon: Multnomah Publishers, Inc., 2005.

Native Wisdom for White Minds: Daily Reflections Inspired by the Native Peoples of the World by Anne Wilson Schaef, Ph.D. New York: Ballentine Books, 1995.
Prayers: A Communion With Our Creator by Don Miguel Ruiz, M.D. and Janet Mills. California: Amber-Allen Publishing, 2001.

The Promise of Wisdom by Rachel Schwandt. Florida: Sourcebooks, Inc., 2002.

Quilt Pieces by Mary Willete Hughes. Minnesota: Minnesota North Star Press of St. Cloud, Inc., 2001.

The Quotable Mom, Kate Rowinsky, Ed. Connecticut: The Lyons Press, 2002.

Stories for The Teacher's Heart by Alice Gray, Ed. Oregon: Multnomah Publishers, Inc., 2002.

Synergy: Connecting to the Power of Cooperation (The Portable 7 Habits), by Stephen Covey and Tammy Smith. Salt Lake City: Franklin Covey Co., 2000.

Thoughts to Share With a Wonderful Son by Douglas Pagels Ed. Colorado: Blue Mountain Arts, 1999. Also by Blue Mountain Arts: *Thoughts to Share With a Wonderful Daughter; a Wonderful Mother; a Wonderful Father; a Wonderful Friend.*

Words of Wisdom: A Book of Inspiration by Armand Eisen, Missouri: Andrews McMeel Publishing, 2001.

Books With Questions for Circle Rounds

How Far Will You Go? Questions to Test Your Limits by Evelyn McFarlane & James Saywell. New York: Villard Books, 1999.

How You Do Anything Is How You Do Everything: A Workbook, A Hands-On Write-Draw-Color-Paint-Cut-Paste Workbook Designed to Assist In the Process of Self-discovery by Cheri Huber & June Shiver. California: Keep It Simple Books, 1988.

If...Questions for the Game of Life by Evelyn McFarlane & James Saywell. New York: Villard Books, 1995.

If...500 New Questions for the Game of Life by Evelyn McFarlane & James Saywell. New York: Villard Books, 1996.

If...Questions for the Game of Love by Evelyn McFarlane & James Saywell. New York: Villard Books, 1998.

If...Questions for the Soul by Evelyn McFarlane & James Saywell, New York: Villard Books, 1998.

Kidchat: Questions to Fuel Young Minds and Mouths by Bret Nicholaus and Paul Lowrie, South Dakota: Questmark Entertainment/Publishing, 2004.

Workshops and Facilitators for Circle Work

Celebration Circles
11934 300 Avenue
Princeton, Minnesota 55371
nancymcc@earthlink.net
sherjw@live.com
763-389-3951 or 763-389-4987
Nancy McCreight and Sherry Winter facilitate circles and teach workshops to hold circles that honor and celebrate life.

PeerSpirit, Inc.
PO Box 550
Langley, Washington 98260
360-331-3580
www.peerspirit.com
Christina Baldwin and Ann Linnea are dedicated to bringing circle into mainstream culture. They offer practicums and wilderness adventures for organizations and personal growth. Rotating leadership, sharing responsibility and attending to the sacred are the cornerstones to their circle training that fits all uses of circle in our culture.

Sarah MacDougall Ed.D.
Maribec Coaching and Consulting
PeerSpirit Practitioner
755 West Street
Taylors Falls, MN 55084
651-428-3104
sarah@maribec.com
Sarah is president of the board for Calling the Circle Foundation, a non-profit dedicated to furthering knowledge of circle as a modern form of social interaction. The board website is http://callingthecircle.org which contains information on circle-based organizations. There are two video clips embedded from You Tube that teach about circle process.

Heartland Inc.
4234 Grimes Avenue South
Edina, Minnesota 55416
952-925-5995
www.heartlandcircle.com
Patricia and Craig Neal created Essential Conversations for individuals and organizations to use in bringing about systematic change needed in these extraordinary times. Using the Principles of Essential Conversations, The Art of Convening Trainings are designed for Workshop and Group Facilitators and Trainers to transform your meetings and conversations.

The Council Process
The Ojai Foundation
9739 Ojai-Santa Paula Road
Ojai, California 93023
www.ojaifoundation.org
Jack Zimmerman, Virginia Coyle and staff offer circle council training for family, schools and organizations. Jack Zimmerman launched a council based, human development curriculum for students ages twelve through eighteen at Crossroads School in Santa Monica, California in 1983. The school council program offers a safe environment that allows students a voice and a place to address issues and concerns and is now implemented in numerous schools.

Circle Web Sites

Christina Baldwin and Ann Linnea's PeerSpirit Practicums for personal growth and organizations:
www.peerspirit.com

Wisdom Circles: Self Discovery and Community Building in Small Group:
www.wisdomcircle.org

Heartland Inc.: Patricia and Craig Neal use the circle format for organizational growth and change:
www.heartlandcircle.com

Jack Zimmerman, Virginia Coyle and staff offer circle council training for family, schools and other settings. The Ojai Foundation:
www.ojaifoundation.org

Mettanokit is a non-profit learning center and service organization highlighting the work of Manitonquat using circles in prisons:
www.circleway.org

The Co-Intelligence Institute on Circles:
www.co-intelligence.org/P-listeningcircles.html

Study Circles Resource Center: Matt Leighninger introduces the use of study circles for community issues:
www.everyday-democracy.org

The "Talking Stick" Circle: An Ancient Tool For Better Decision Making And Strengthening Community. George Por speaks on circles for community and organizations:
http://world.std.com/~lo/95.05/0114.html

Many Thanks

Nancy:

Many thanks to my circle teachers Harold Gatensby, Mark Wedge, Kay Pranis and Barry Stuart. When I listen, everyone is a potential teacher as was Pat Carini who helped me see the gifts and possibilities in each of us.

I am grateful to my daughter Emily for her endless love and endearing energetic spirit, my husband Jon for his encouragement and my family and friends for their years of inspiration. My deep appreciation goes to my parents, Guy and Helen Miller, for their unconditional love, which continues to be a deep well from which I draw. Finally, to my co-author Sherry, thanks for your honest and loving heart and the endless supply of tea, chocolate and good will as, together we practiced the art of collaboration and grew our friendship.

Sherry:

I have many teachers to acknowledge for my wonderful journey with circles: Harold Gatensby and Mark Wedge for introducing me to circle, Christina Baldwin and Ann Linnea from PeerSpirit for expanding my skills in circle facilitation and opening my heart to a new way, Tom Nolan and Lola Rae Long from The Ojai Foundation for giving me insight on using circles for youth, Craig and Patricia Neal from Heartland Institute for providing the opportunity to experience circles for organizational growth and Pat and Judge Steve Ruble for inviting me to be a part of Peacemaking Circles.

I thank my husband Larry for his support, daughters Chris and Lisa for their compassion and inspiration and my grandsons Bryce, Dylan and granddaughters Alexandra and Maya, all who continually surprise me with their sense of wonder and understanding of spirit.

A special thank you to dear friend Nancy for her patience and welcoming everything about my nature.

Nancy and Sherry:

Together, we thank the following people for sharing their circle stories and experiences: Sherri Gutkaes, Sandy Haehn, Jane Hanson, Sandi Hanson, Sharon Hanson, Connie Hodder, Steve Hodder, Brenda Hoffman, Jon and Emily McCreight, Bonnie Nelson, Linda Odegard, Carole Orton, Lorraine Orton, Bryce Potvin, Marcia Ruise, Eileen Sanborn, Deborah Sorenson, Jodi Sternquist, Catherine Watson, Karen Wilson, and Margaret Woodward.

Additional thanks to those who read manuscript drafts: Barbara Blackstone, Carolyn and Chris Bornhauser, Denise Breton, Carol Larsen, Shelley Larson, Sarah MacDougall, Jon McCreight, Patricia and Craig Neal, Linda Odegard, Carole and David Orton, Kay Pranis, Marcia Ruise, Deborah Sorenson, Ellie Slette, Robin Suhsen, Jim Tomsky and Karen Wilson.

About the Authors

Nancy McCreight is a mediator and facilitator with extensive circle training and experience including workshops with First Nation trainers from Canada's Yukon and circle authors, Kay Pranis and Barry Stuart. She was a program coordinator for communities using Peacemaking Circles and a researcher on a nation wide project involving circles. She holds a Master's Degree in Educational Psychology.

Sherry Winter is a writer, business owner, photographer, and circle facilitator. She obtained her Master of Human Development degree with a focus on the circle process, training with Community Justice Circle teachers from the Yukon, PeerSpirit Circling and The Ojai Foundation and has facilitated circles for Community Justice, retreats, life celebrations, house warmings, Solstices and other celebrations.

Nancy and Sherry have facilitated and participated in over one hundred circles and continue to be renewed and amazed by the power of sharing life's experiences and stories.

Blessings, Nancy and Sherry

Printed in the United States
151253LV00001B/135/P